I AM WITH YOU

Words of comfort & strength for difficult times

STELLA TOMLINSON

Soul Forge Press

Copyright © 2023 Stella Tomlinson

All rights reserved. This book or parts thereof may not be reproduced in any form, stored in any retrieval system, or transmitted in any form by any means – electronic, mechanical, photocopy, recording, or otherwise – without prior written permission of the author, except in the case of brief quotations embodied in reviews and certain other non-commercial uses permitted by copyright law.

Published by Soul Forge Press 2023.

ISBN 978-1-7393291-0-5

I Am With You is also available in ebook format:
ISBN 978-1-7393291-1-2

First edition.

Book cover and internal design by the author.

Cover and internal images by Veronika Oliinyk / ID 1286698246 / iStock

The poems 'You Will Not Silence Me' and 'Come Back to Your Heart' have previously been published in *Cycles of Belonging* by Stella Tomlinson (Womancraft Publishing 2022).

Visit the author's website at: stellatomlinson.com

The information given in this book is for reference only and is not a substitute for professional medical advice: always consult a professional / medical practitioner. Any use of the information in this book is at the reader's risk and discretion. The author assumes no responsibility or liability for any injuries or losses that may result.

CONTENTS

OPENING WORDS 1

    WHEN DARKNESS CALLS 4

    EVER-CHANGING CYCLES 7

    THE HEART OF OUR PAIN 9

    SUPPORTIVE RESOURCES 15

    LINGERING WITH LONGING 19

    SOUL GUIDANCE 20

    MY WISH FOR YOU 22

PROLOGUE: INANNA'S DESCENT 25

BEGIN (& END) HERE: WITH SELF-COMPASSION 27

DESCENDING 29

    LET GO (I) 32

        Fear of letting go 33

    WHEN DARKNESS CALLS (I) 34

        Hearing the call 35

    I AM WITH YOU 36

        The community of all things 37

    DESCENDING 38

        An invitation 39

    UNRAVELLING 40

        Unravel the threads 41

    SOME DAYS 42

        Be a friend to yourself 43

    DEATH MOTHER 46

        The inner critic 47

    STONE 50

        Being with what is 52

    GRIEF MOVES 54

How to feel 55
HEALING WATERS 56
The healing power of tears 57
A QUESTION 58
Living your own life 59
BRUISED 60
Soul whispers 61
ASHES 62
Honouring anger 63
UNBOUND 66
Unwinding 67
PORTAL 68
Grief as a portal 69
THE SCAR 70
Tending your wounds 71
A BLESSING FROM THE DEPTHS 72

IN THE WINTRY UNDERWORLD 73

WHEN DARKNESS CALLS (II) 76
The gifts of darkness 77
WASTELAND 78
Your inner landscape 79
LIMINAL 82
Unanswered questions 83
I DON'T KNOW 84
Not knowing 86
VERNALIZATION 88
Emotional seasons 89
WINTERING 90
Inner winters 91
REST IN ME 94
Your body as refuge 95
LET ME ASSURE YOU 96
Boundaries 97

SHE WHISPERS	98
On feeling held	99
LET GO (II)	102
Letting yourself let go	103
HOW TO GRIEVE	106
On grieving	107
STRONG FOUNDATIONS	108
Self-worth	109
ASK YOURSELF THIS	112
How do you feel & what do you need?	113
SEARING	116
Go gently	117
COURAGE	118
Your courageous heart	119
THE FORGE	120
On smithcraft	121
LOST AND FOUND	122
Finding yourself	123
THE FLAME	124
Surrendering	125
REASONS TO KEEP GOING	126
Look around you	127
HEART FIRE	130
Sourcing love	131
THE COMPANY I KEEP	132
Sacred nature	133
EARTHED	136
The Great Mother	137
YOU ARE HEALING	138
What is healing?	139
THE BUD	142
On hope	143
A PRAYER	144
On prayer	145

RETURNING 147

THIS MUCH I KNOW 150
Speaking your truth 152
SOME PEOPLE 154
You are needed 155
LESSONS 156
Acceptance 157
NAMING THE PARTS 160
The inner family 161
LET GO (III) 162
The gift of letting go..163
RETURNING 166
Mothering yourself 167
AND THEN 170
Start the day this way 171
RIP UP THE SCRIPT 172
Whose life is it anyway?..173
HER SOUL IS ABLAZE 176
Rising from the ashes..177
SOUL FIRE 178
The fire element 179
BRIGHT BEACON 182
The power of anger 183
SOLAR POWERED 184
Adult life skills 185
RESIST 188
Patriarchy 189
NICE GIRL NO MORE 192
On niceness 193
ONE MORNING..196
The power of saying 'fuck it' 197
HAVE YOU HEARD HER? 198
Your untamed soul self 199

- You Will Not Silence Me 202
  - Remember your ancestresses 203
- Birdsong 204
  - Authentic expression 205
- My Song 206
  - Your untamed voice 208
- The Soul of the Rose 210
  - Purpose and calling 211
- Some Good Facts 214
  - Taking in the good 215
- Dwelling Place 218
  - Default mode 219
- This Is How I Live 220
  - Living in the mystery 221
- Come Back To Your Heart 222
  - Heart power 224
- Home 226
  - Coming home 227
- Wings 228
  - The chrysalis opens 229
- A Blessing of Renewal 230

CLOSING PRAYER 231

WHAT NEXT 233

ACKNOWLEDGEMENTS 234

ABOUT THE AUTHOR 235

OPENING WORDS

Let me begin by promising you this.

Dear one, you are not alone.

No matter how life has battered you; no matter how bruised your heart feels; no matter how confused your mind is. You are not alone.

You are not alone in your sorrow, your grief, your confusion, or your sadness. You are not alone when you feel down, when you feel like giving up, or when you just cannot see the next step or the way out. You are not alone even if you feel utterly overwhelmed by your emotions and that no-one understands you.

Yes, you may feel lost. But you are not alone.

I am with you, and I know how it feels.

So, if you feel like this today, or have ever felt like this – please, please understand, that you are *not* alone.

While I can't wave a magic wand and take away the feelings, I can offer you the knowledge that other people feel this way too. That you're not the only person to feel what you feel so intensely. I feel it too. As do millions upon millions of fellow deep-feeling souls out there in the world.

It is valuable to realise that despite the messages you may have received from this superficial soulless mainstream culture we live in, it is natural and it is okay to feel challenging emotions such as anger, sorrow and heartache.

Because part of being human is to experience loss and grief and doubt (and wonder and contentment and joy too).

Perhaps you can find solace in the thought that your tendency to feel challenging emotions intensely comes with the ability to feel awe and fun and love and radiant happiness much more profoundly too.

It is human to feel deeply.

Yet how many of us truly share our pain with others? How many of us put on a brave face instead and soldier on, despite the burden of the emotional pain we're carrying?

And how many of us more deep-feeling souls attempt to bury our intense feelings to try and fit in because we've been told we're too sensitive, should develop a thicker skin and stop being so dramatic?

Too many, I'd say.

We all experience difficult times.

Things happen that leave us feeling insecure, confused, angry, wounded, overwhelmed, unsafe, sad, grieving, numb or fearful. We may experience periods of anxiety, low mood, maybe depression.

And all of these are natural human emotions, arising in response to experiencing difficult times.

But too often we feel lonely in our sadness, isolated in our anxiety, and abandoned when we feel down. We see the smiling faces and apparently perfect lives of our friends, associates and celebrities on social media and we feel shut out as if there's something wrong with us for not being able to move on or keep calm and carry on.

I know how lonely this can feel because I have felt that way too.

I know how the pain of confusion, grief and doubt can feel immensely challenging – overwhelming even.

And though I may not be using the same words as you to describe how you feel, can you find solace in knowing that here, as you read, there is another soul speaking to you, who also feels the challenges of being human?

Can you find comfort in my reaching out to you to say:

'It hurts, I know. I feel you. I hear you. It's okay to not feel okay. It's human. It's natural for your emotions to ebb and flow; to rise up and to spiral down. Life can be hard on a tender heart and a sensitive soul. I am with you in this. I understand'.

I know it helps me, when my heart feels heavy, to remember that this is all part of our common humanity. To truly live means to feel deeply. Both the sorrow *and* the joy; the pain *and* the bliss; the grief *and* the love. All of it. Ever-changing, just like the seasons, just like the moon.

And so, through the words in this book, may I offer you many more reminders that I am with you, and that you are not alone?

And may these words remind you that even though, at times, you may feel lost, it *is* possible to rediscover the good in yourself and the joy of life.

WHEN DARKNESS CALLS

I wrote the poems you will find here during a period in my life when I decided to surrender to the grief, anger and sorrow I had been struggling with, in truth, for many years.

Well, I say I 'decided'. It would be more realistic to say that I arrived at a fork in the path of my life. I could either continue along the route of swallowing my anger, numbing my grief, and being overcome by anxiety or I could surrender to what needed to be felt and let it in, up and through.

I chose the challenging path of surrender.

In the preceding years I had done much work – with a therapist and through my own personal development and psycho-spiritual practices – to meet, understand and offer compassion to the wounded inner child within me who had not received the unconditional love, affirmation, emotional support and holding she needed from her parents to feel safe, seen and fundamentally worthy. As a result, I had been struggling though life with a painful sense of never feeling good enough.

Along the way I had been to dark places where I wished I could just close my eyes and fade away. I'd experienced numb dullness, my inner landscape filled with a grey mist that made it impossible to see or feel clearly. I'd been so anxious that my throat clamped shut, I couldn't catch hold of my breath and I'd lose sense of my feet, whole body throbbing, head full of crackly static.

But the insistent urge that I tend to the inner wounded child within me kept me going. I knew she was crucial to my wellbeing. I wouldn't abandon or reject her as she had been before. I wouldn't hurt her again. I could feel how she needed someone to be there for her and to love her, and I knew that person had to be me.

I came to understand that it was essential I found ways to be with and process my grief and anger so I could free 'Little Stella' from her prison of shame. I needed to believe in my essential goodness, root into self-worth and own my right to express the truth of my experiences and feelings. Only then would she finally feel seen and supported enough to relax so I could move forward with my life.

It is no coincidence that I was also in the rite of passage that is midlife and the peri/menopause transition. This is a time when darkness calls and demands that we turn inwards and descend to tend to our deepest hurts and wounds. A time we are called to enter the soul forge to be transformed on the anvil of an extended inner autumn and winter – a symbolic death of the old constricted, conditioned, wounded self – in order to be reborn.

By early 2022 I had arrived at a point where I had dug deeply and found myself closer and closer to the roots of my pain. I realised it was time to stop digging and to sit with what I had unearthed and to let myself feel the anger, the disappointment and frustration as well as the sorrow, loss and heartache that were yearning to be acknowledged and listened to.

And as I sat with all of this, a calm presence descended, and words began to arise. Words from my soul. Words from source. Words from the Great Mother – which is what I call the spiritual presence who is there through life's cycles of birth, growth, death and rebirth.

The poems you will read here are expressions of what I discovered when I sat with my complex and challenging feelings. And the accompanying reflections share with you some of the practices that have helped me and lessons I have learned along my healing path.

In receiving and writing these words, and in reading them to myself many, many times, I have found them to be a source of comfort and solace; of hope, healing and inspiration.

And now I share them with you so that you may feel affirmed and validated in your own difficult times and know there is someone there with you who understands.

EVER-CHANGING CYCLES

I know how it is to feel lost, abandoned, isolated or misunderstood. This can be a lonely place.

But how would it be to understand that these challenging times are part of the inevitable experience of a life fully lived? And that they are part of the natural rhythm of life?

For life is cyclic.

The moon waxes and wanes. The year moves through the seasons as the wheel of the year is ever turning. Those of us who menstruate experience our monthly cycle – as well as the larger lifecycle of menarche (first bleed), menstruation and then menopause. We travel through youth into maturity and into old age.

We are cyclic beings.

Change is the natural state of life: it is *our* natural state.

When we understand life to be a constant spiral of cycles and seasons, then perhaps we can reappraise our times of emotional darkness as inner winters. A natural fallow phase of the cycle of life that does not last forever.

Just as spring follows winter, your inner emotional landscape will shift and change and new shoots of hope will return; seeds of joy will grow, bud and bloom.

Life has its own rhythm. And, just as we cannot force the spring flowers to appear before they are ready, perhaps we should ease off trying to force ourselves to be happy and content all the time, especially when there are very real and valid strong and challenging emotions coursing through our inner landscape.

Perhaps our difficulty with granting ourselves permission to feel and process loss, grief and doubt is because these are wintry experiences that call us to retreat, slow down, turn inwards and listen to our feelings and needs so we might better repair our wounded places and bruised hearts.

And this feels counterintuitive to our culture which values the expansive outgoing energies of spring and summer above all. We feel the pressure to be sociable and active, to grow and advance, to be positive and open, to be consistently available, and to care for others and put their needs above our own (particularly those of us who are socialised as women).

We are conditioned to feel acceptable only when exhibiting spring and summer energies of creating, achieving and producing.

We berate ourselves when we cannot be constantly productive.

We're conditioned to keep calm and carry on with a smile on our face.

We often don't have the language to describe our feelings.

We are not given permission to be angry or sad. Anger is swallowed down. And too often we are medicated to silence our grief and sadness rather than being given the time, space and compassionate holding to explore what lies beneath them.

But this is not the way of life. Day always turns to night. The moon wanes. Winter comes every year.

When we do not – or cannot – answer the call to retreat and repair, our inner winters become particularly savage: freezing and tumultuous like being lost in a snowstorm or tossed around by a howling gale.

Our feelings may end up overwhelming us because the emotional pain does not disappear. We may think we can push the feelings away and bottle them up ... but they *will* make themselves known whether through dis-ease or explosive emotional outbursts. Either way, it makes a mess.

So let us reappraise our difficult times as periods of winter in our life, which may well feel challenging, but have their own rhythm and flow.

THE HEART OF OUR PAIN

The more and more I feel into my own hurt and heartache the more I realise that what lies beneath it all is grief.

The more and more I reflect on my emotional struggles and difficult times the more I can sense how, at their core, is a loss of some kind and the sorrow and heartache that comes with loss.

What do you think of when I talk of grief?

Perhaps you think of bereavement – the loss of a loved one, friend, or a beloved pet and the agonising heartbreak that comes with this. Or maybe the death of someone who meant a lot to you but perhaps you didn't personally know, such as a public figure you loved and respected. And alongside this you may also mourn the loss of the hopes you had for the person and what they meant to you in your life.

This kind of loss can arrive like a lightning strike and bring grief flooding into our lives: a tempest of emotion that can be overwhelming. And it may linger like the bleakest grey wintry sky, sitting heavily in our hearts.

Culturally, this is what we tend to think of when we speak of grief. But there are other losses we grieve during our lives, whether we realise it or not. And even if we don't use the word 'grief', its energy weighs heavily on our hearts; a burden of sadness we carry that we long to be able to set down.

There are personal losses through partings and estrangements from friends, family, and romantic partners.

There is the loss of money or financial stability and the subsequent lack of security.

Changes in circumstances can lead to a loss of identity, free time or a sense of freedom or agency, even if they are changes you'd sought out, such as parenthood or a promotion at work. Or loss of identity can arrive through circumstances beyond your control such as being made redundant from work.

We each experience disappointments or betrayals by people we once trusted. Other times we lose faith in others such as community members, teachers or leaders. We might even lose faith in ourselves.

Or you might arrive at a point in your life where you've achieved what you'd set out to, perhaps career-wise, but the realisation dawns that the life you've created no longer fits: this is no longer who you are anymore.

And, as time goes on, there may be the aching realisation of opportunities lost and the fading of hopes, dreams and expectations.

Then there is mourning the fading of youth; loss of health; changes to mental faculties.

And while each loss is unique to us in what happens and how it lands, the experience of loss is universal – it is part of our common humanity.

There's an old and touching story from the Buddhist tradition that teaches us this universal truth:

In the time of the Buddha, there lived a woman called Kisa Gotami. After losing her precious only child, Kisa Gotami became desperate and asked if anyone could help her. Her sorrow was so great that many thought she had lost her mind.

An old man told her to see the Buddha who, in turn, told her that he could bring the child back to life if she could find white mustard seeds from a family where no one had died.

She desperately went from house to house, but to her disappointment, she could not find a house that had not suffered the death of a family member.

Finally, the realisation struck her that there is no house free from mortality and, still sad but knowing that her sorrow was shared, she found a sense of peace with her loss.[1]

---

[1] Adapted from en.wikipedia.org/wiki/Kisa_Gotami

In addition to personal grief, we may experience feelings of loss and sorrow when we look at what is happening in the world. For example, when we see negative changes in our neighbourhood or severing of community links; the closing of much-needed services and dismantling of support systems; or the loss of faith in leaders who do not live up to the standards in public life we expect and need.

We watch the news and see instances of injustice and violence and may feel the pain of it as if it were our own.

And there is the grief that arises from the impact of racism, misogyny, ableism, cis-heteronormativity, and the manifold ways humans have been and still are cruel, hateful and violent to those we individually or culturally other.

There is the grief of these times of loss we are living in: whether through the COVID-19 pandemic or the loss that cuts through bonds with family and friends when tightly held opinions differ and we cannot find consensus, as well as the sorrow caused by increasing polarisation and the accompanying loss of nuance, patience and compassion in this post-truth age.

And then there is the wider loss of environmental diversity: we may experience ecological grief – anguish and sorrow (and perhaps outrage too) – for the destruction of habitats and the delicate ecosystems that support life on Earth.

Finally, if this resonates with your beliefs and experience, there may be a grief about being here on Earth in human form – a kind of exile from the Oneness of spirit.

These are just some of the many losses and griefs of which we may be consciously aware or that may be unconsciously troubling our hearts.

And so, while our own inner emotional landscape may be complex and varied, or possibly numb and barren, perhaps each of us in our own way is, when we get to the heart of it, grieving something that has been lost, or that never was but we wish it might have been.

It is a lot. It can feel almost too much to bear. Relentless.

For in our culture, we are not taught how to grieve; we are not taught how to be with our feelings wisely and skilfully.

Of all the losses I listed above – all of which generate very real and tangible sorrow and heartache – how many of them are culturally recognised?

Not many.

And when these losses are not seen and affirmed by our culture, we may reject our own feelings and push away the energy which is calling to be expressed. Especially when in the past (or even present) we've been told we're too sensitive.

Our hearts close off and become armoured. We withdraw from pain and in doing so we also withdraw from joy as our range of available feelings shrinks to a tiny spectrum of numbness.

Yet still the grief will find us. It is part of the air we are breathing. It is human to feel sorrow. There is much to mourn in our own individual life and in these times we are living in. It is not negative to say this; it is simply to name the truth of human experience.

*

Dear reader, like me you yearn to live with an open heart. But how to do this without it being bruised and battered, again and again?

I believe we need to develop courage to engage with this world with an open heart. But we also need the wisdom to discern when it is best to withdraw for a while and to lick our wounds and rest … so we might build up the courage and strength to re-engage with the world once again.

The foundation of living with an open heart is to courageously speak the truth of how we are feeling.

This begins with mustering the courage to engage with our *own* heart and mind and the shadowy places within our psyche where our angry, jealous and grieving parts have been pushed away from our conscious recognition.

To do this, we must first learn to be aware of *how* we are feeling: an essential life skill that seems a radically simple idea but is one that you may find curiously challenging. Especially as when we're in overwhelm we can shut down our feeling capacity to try and function in the world.

This can feel vulnerable. But it is only when you are aware of how you are feeling that the necessary alchemy can take place that allows the emotional pain to dissipate.

After all, the word 'emotion' comes from the Latin *e-movere*, which means 'to move out', so our emotions can be reframed as 'energy in motion': it is energy that *needs* to move through you.

Ignored emotions get trapped and cause further pain; felt emotions will, eventually, shift and change. Their pain *will* lessen.

And once you recognise your stress, pain, weariness or grief you may well find that a natural compassion towards yourself arises: a kind-hearted recognition that, yes, things feel hard for you right now; yes, you are suffering; yes, you want to help yourself feel better; and yes, you *are* going to help yourself feel better.

How would it feel to offer yourself the heartfelt tender wish that this suffering will ease; that you will find a greater peace?

Perhaps by opening this book you have already begun to summon the courage to be with your challenging feelings and to offer yourself the healing balm of self-compassion…

SUPPORTIVE RESOURCES

Our capacity to cope with challenging feelings can, at least in part, be determined by the supportive resources we have available to us. And these can be both externally and internally sourced.

Let's consider external resources first.

Who do you have in your life who supports you already? Perhaps a partner, family, friends, neighbours, colleagues, acquaintances. Even if they do not always give you as much support as you'd like, how would it be to acknowledge the felt sense of their presence and the support they *do* give you? The practical things they do that help you, the companionship, the camaraderie, the love.

Consider teachers and guides from whom you learn – whether spiritual or secular. Think about writers, course providers or content producers whose work you read or listen to and value and whose knowledge or wisdom sustains you in some way. These are all forms of support available to you now.

There are nourishing and healing activities that you might enjoy such as cooking, crafting, writing, walking – satisfying pursuits that support you by providing respite from the crazy world, and maybe also a sense of calm or peace.

Step outside and notice the support of the ground beneath your feet. Be aware of standing on the earth that grows your food and of the sun shining down sustaining you and all life on this planet.

And beyond this practical support, there is the beauty of the natural world that feeds your soul – the radiance and scent of flowers, the heart-lifting song of birds, the ever-shifting unique formations of the clouds in the sky.

While outer resources such as these are vital and significant, we can also experience and grow *inner* resources of the *felt sense* of support.

For example, notice the chair you are sitting on and the points of contact between it and your body – and sense how it feels within your body and mind to receive this support; to feel held and safe and still in this moment.

Become aware, if you can, of the presence of your bones and spine and invite an inner feeling of dignity and strength.

Notice there is more than enough air to breathe, and with each breath open to feeling sustained and supported – this air enables you to move, speak and to live.

Your heart is beating – 100,000 times a day – without you needing to do a thing about it.

Your internal organs are performing millions of essential processes every second to keep you alive – no matter the level of health you're currently experiencing.

And gravity is always holding you.

At a spiritual level, you might call on whatever presence speaks to you. Perhaps Mother Earth, God or Goddess. Perhaps Great Spirit or good ancestors. Maybe guides or angels. Let their presence hold you and cradle you.

And, at the most wide-ranging view, open to the awareness of time and space. The support offered through being held by the cycles of the moon and the seasons. How would it be to open to awareness of the ever-flowing ongoingness of existence and the living cosmos? Such awareness, if it resonates, can feel tremendously supportive and offers a broader perspective to personal troubles.

Can you imagine moving through your day with the felt sense and presence of being supported?

What relief that would bring!

All these sources of support help you to feel less alone and in turn can help you *be* with strong feelings or overwhelming experiences.

Because the more you feel supported the more you will be able to carry the load of your grief, doubt, regret, confusion or sorrow.

The more you can recognise the support that is already available to you the more you will be able to open your heart and find the courageous vulnerability you need to be with your feelings.

This is a vital life skill.

For when you have the capacity and skills to be with your challenging feelings the more settled you will feel within yourself.

When you can sit with your pain and heartache, you will be more at ease with yourself for you will know yourself better.

You will feel more grounded and centred so when the next tempest arrives, as it surely will, you will have a solid place to which to return – no matter how far off course the gale has blown you.

May the words in this book help you to sit with your emotional struggles with a tender heart. And may you experience the alchemy of this pain turning to kindness and compassion.

Because in doing the hard work of sitting with your pain you will become more self-compassionate and develop a gentle warm-hearted intimacy with yourself.

And in turn you will likely become more tender-hearted and kinder to others because you feel our common humanity, united in our experience of sorrow.

You will be trusted because others will intuitively sense this ground within you.

May you come to embody and radiate the wisdom that none of us is alone.

Opening Words

LINGERING WITH LONGING

I wonder whether you'd agree that there is an aspect of human nature that is drawn towards melancholy?

And that this is particularly pronounced in those of us who are of a more sensitive, deep-feeling disposition.

Some people are drawn to lingering with heartache and sorrow; to dwelling in poignancy and longing … while others run as quickly as they can in the opposite direction from it!

But for us wistful souls (and I include myself here and you too as you've been drawn to this book), well, we long to recover a lost spiritual connection and to come home to something bigger than ourselves with deeper meaning; to merge with something that both transcends this human experience *and* roots us deeply into life on Earth.

There's a Welsh word that captures this sense of longing: *hiraeth*[2]. There's no equivalent word in English. It means nostalgia, yearning, longing; a desire for something which feels just out of reach. A beautifully evocative word for a concept that is delightfully poignant and resonant.

This inclination towards longing has been called a 'bittersweet' outlook on life[3] and it is tender and quite beautiful in its own way. Engaging with sorrow and yearning adds subtlety, depth and texture to life; qualities sensitive souls by nature enjoy.

---

[2] Pronounced *'here-eyeth'* with a rolled 'r'. (By the way, I lived in Wales for 8 years and my husband is Welsh.)

[3] By Susan Cain in her book *Bittersweet: How Sorrow and Longing Make Us Whole.*

I consider this bittersweet outlook a beautiful gift of feeling deeply, because when we engage with our heartache and sorrow and sink into their complex depths, we learn more about ourselves and the human condition.

We dive beneath the surface of life and swim in its fascinating yet mysterious depths and over time come to understand life at a more complex level – including ourselves. And when we engage with what's going on in our subconscious, we're more likely to heal any pain at its root.

Perhaps dark nights of the soul are familiar territory to those of us who value poignancy, precisely because we experience life so intensely – we cannot ignore our own pain and we cannot ignore the pain of others.

However, this doesn't make life easy. Because when other people are splashing around contentedly in the shallows of life it can feel lonely and confusing to heed the call to disappear for a while and dive into the murky depths that lie beneath the surface.

But we also know these deep dives are worth it for the pearls of wisdom we shall uncover and for the satisfaction of knowing we are living an authentic and meaningful life.

So let us follow our longings and may they lead us home.

SOUL GUIDANCE

Throughout this book I mention the word *soul*.

Now I do not presume to tell you what your soul means to you, but for clarity this is what I mean when I speak of 'soul'.

Opening Words

When I speak of the 'soul' I am talking about your essential self. Your deepest self. That part of you which knows.

I view the soul as the unique combination of your temperament, aptitudes, values, preferences *and* the gifts you were born to share with the world. It's the true you. The real you.

While our *spirit* may be considered the transcendent part of us that is connected to the Oneness of all things, our *soul* calls us inwards to connect to and live from what is most unique in us.

While *spirit* calls us to rise and transcend our sense of self, *soul* calls us to descend into our bodies and root ourselves in the truth of who we are and engage with our emotions and feelings ... and listen to the wild call of our yearnings and longings – the messy but beautiful truths of our inner nature.

For me, as well as it being the animating, immaterial, ineffable and sacred spark that is each of us as an individual, your soul is also a unique expression of life living itself which connects us back to the web of life of all living things.

Your soul is your essential self, and it has a calling.

It speaks through images and whispers and symbols. It is heard in your longings and yearnings and drives your search for purpose and meaning. It's in that intuitive feeling you have when you just know something is right or wrong for you.

It is expansive... Numinous... Sacred... Mysterious...

It asks us to heal our emotional pain and see beyond the everyday grind and grievances; it asks us to move past the limits and conditioning of our upbringing and to challenge the prevailing myths, life-denying agendas and soulless distractions of the prevailing culture.

It nudges us to follow our longings so we may contribute our unique note to the song of life for the good of all.

I believe that our soul is always whispering to us … but we need to make space to hear it.

And so each poem here is followed by a piece that invites you to reflect further on its theme. Together these poems and reflections offer an invitation to dive deeper, beyond the everyday mind that judges and frets and plans and analyses, and experience the intuitive insight and wisdom that lies beneath the surface: the wisdom of your soul.

Because you will be on the right path when you allow your soul to guide you.

MY WISH FOR YOU

Dear one, life will always be challenging.

The human condition is to love and lose, to soar high with joy and to sink low with grief – and all the myriad of emotional states in between.

The trick is to find ways to cope with the ups and downs.

To remember to savour and truly appreciate the joys without clinging onto them, because you appreciate that they will not last forever.

To weather the emotional storms without drowning in them because you realise that they too will pass.

Opening Words

Life is cyclic and change is our natural state. Life has its own rhythm.

There is much wisdom in truly coming to understand this and in courageously feeling all your feelings knowing that inner winters need to be experienced before spring can return.

And so with the poems, reflections, practices and questions I am sharing with you here, my wish for you is that you will feel less alone with challenging feelings and in difficult times.

They're words of comfort and strength for times when you're struggling and feeling down; times when grief, sorrow, regret or low self-worth are weighing heavily on your heart; times when you need some words of solace and hope, motivation and inspiration; and times when you need the friendly voice of someone who understands to both affirm your feelings *and* help you find perspective.

All parts of you are welcome here, dear one.

I hope that you can feel my presence with you as you read this book, and that you will realise that you are not alone in experiencing despair or sadness, bitterness or heartache so powerfully. I am with you in spirit as we journey through this challenging and enchanting experience that is a human life. I am with you in the common thread that binds us all: grief and love.

Let me be a companion speaking to you through these pages, offering you comfort and compassion, inspiration and strength. I hope you might feel the warmth of my hand gently placed on yours, and my consoling arm wrapped around your shoulders.

May these words offer balm for your heart and give you permission to feel deeply, whatever your mood. May you remember that shutting down your emotions leads to a dreary life. If you can open to sadness and grief, then you will likely experience delight and joy more intensely.

I offer each piece as a word potion: good medicine to bring you the self-compassion and healing you're perhaps longing for.

Read, receive and let these words work their magic in your soul. And whenever you find yourself consumed by wintry darkness, may these words be there for you, offering a flame of solace, warmth, hope and courage.

May you feel the spark of recognition when a piece speaks to how you're feeling.

May you feel seen and affirmed.

May you feel the tender glow of self-compassion warming your heart and spreading through your body and consoling and healing the wounded places within you.

And, in realising that it is human to experience life's losses, pains and challenges, and that you are not alone in your suffering, may you feel the strength of this common humanity holding you and encouraging you so that you need never feel alone again.

Stella Tomlinson
Hampshire, UK,
December 2022

PROLOGUE: INANNA'S DESCENT

This book's structure is inspired by the 4,000-year-old Sumerian myth of *The Descent of Inanna*: a story of descent and return via a visit to the underworld:

Inanna, Queen of Heaven, decides to descend to the Underworld to visit her sister Ereshkigal, Queen of the Dead, who is mourning the death of her husband. This displeases Ereshkigal and so as Inanna descends, she is forced to divest herself of each of her seven items of regalia (and her powers).

Then, when Inanna arrives to stand before her sister in the underworld stripped bare, Ereshkigal kills her and hangs her corpse on a hook to rot.

After three days, because she has failed to return, Inanna's personal attendant Ninshubur gets help from two little creatures who travel down into the Underworld and carry the food and water of life to Inanna and secure her release – and they are allowed to do this after empathising with Ereshkigal's grief.

Restored to life Inanna returns to the world above, passing through the seven gates by which she'd descended and reclaims her vestments and powers.

It's a myth symbolic of the journey of the dark night of the soul which drags us into the underworld to meet our own shadows – those difficult and challenging emotions and rejected aspects of our psyche – and where we experience a symbolic and necessary death of our old self so we may be reborn with greater clarity and wisdom.

When we follow the call of the wintry underworld and tend to our heartache and grief we embark on a healing journey that demands we divest ourselves of the elaborate protections that no longer serve us and descend to the death-like force of facing our buried pain, and offer ourselves the healing power of empathy, so we can return to our lives renewed and reclothed having reclaimed what is most vital.

Keep this journey in mind as you read this book. For you will meet the shadowy Ereshkigals of grief and sorrow, who may strip you bare and leave you hanging on the hook.

But do not be afraid because, as this myth shows, offering your shadows empathy and compassion will enable you to imbibe the nourishing soul food and healing waters required to return to life having alchemised your pain into kindness.

And this is what I hope to offer you with the words in this book and this is why it's structured as it is.

First, we **descend** inwards and downwards by acknowledging our painful feelings. Then we find ourselves in the **wintry underworld** of the cave of not-knowing where we may feel abandoned, desolate, even overwhelmed. But here we find that in listening to our feelings they begin to shift and change. We discover deep seams of tender and fierce self-compassion that bring hope and motivation as well as the necessary strength and energy to **return** and re-engage with life with a renewed clarity and vision, a fire in our soul and an open heart.

This is the archetypal journey of descent and return; a journey necessary to achieve emotional maturity and greater self-understanding and acceptance.

It is a journey to encounter your soul.

BEGIN (& END) HERE: WITH SELF-COMPASSION

May I offer you a resource to aid you on your journey?

Touching the tender places of emotional pain and turmoil may trigger frustration, sadness, grief or even anger.

So have this short potent technique at the ready to shift your energy and be kind to yourself.

I invite you to begin with this practice, and to repeat it each time you read some of the words in this book[4].

TAKE A SELF-COMPASSION BREAK

1. Acknowledge the painful feeling

Say something like: 'this is difficult' or 'this feels challenging to acknowledge' or 'this hurts'.

Connect to and acknowledge the feeling – perhaps place a hand over your heart as you mindfully acknowledge it.

2. Connect to a sense of common humanity

Remind yourself that you are not the only person feeling like this. Acknowledging our common humanity can be immensely comforting.

Say to yourself something like: 'I'm not alone in this' or 'other people feel this way too'.

---

[4] Adapted from The Self-Compassion Break by Dr Kristin Neff:
self-compassion.org/exercise-2-self-compassion-break/

With your hands over your heart, feel their warmth and the sensation of kind gentle touch (or whatever soothing touch you might prefer such as placing a hand on your cheek or on your shoulder).

3. Be kind to yourself

Ask yourself, 'What do I need to hear right now to express kindness to myself?'.

For example: 'I'm doing the best I can' or 'may I forgive myself' or 'may I learn to accept myself as I am'.

And now notice how it feels to be kind to yourself.

How does it feel to be warm and tender towards yourself? What sensations are present in your body? Perhaps there's a softening of your eyes, maybe your jaw releases … your shoulders relax. Perhaps there's a spaciousness in your chest… Maybe a warm feeling spreads internally through your abdomen… Maybe your whole body feels more settled … supported.

Notice how offering yourself kindness and compassion feels … and take a few more breaths letting that feeling sink into you as you sink into it... Like a soothing balm or a golden mist settling into your heart … into your bones … into the lonely and hurting places inside you.

Breathe and receive this feeling of kindness into every cell of your being.

DESCENDING

I am angry. And it is burning me up.

I am heavy with grief. And it feels too much to bear.

I am falling. And it feels inevitable.

A force that I cannot resist is pulling me down.

Struggling against it makes it worse.

It wedges me into painful places that bruise my heart and tear at my soul.

But I know it is time to face the truth.

The truth of what has been lost or never was, the opportunities denied, the life (so far) unlived.

The truth of what must be left behind and the truth of what is leaving me.

The truth of what cannot be let go and so must be borne.

The truth of what is to come: the version of me who is demanding to be birthed.

But first I must fall.

First, I must be cracked open as I descend.

My old, over-protected, wounded self is crumbling.

And it hurts.

But I know I must take this journey.

It is time.

And I am ready.

Descending

*

This is the journey of descent.

Here you will find poems and reflections that speak to times when you feel overwhelmed by your emotions; when you feel you are struggling and being pulled under by a force beyond your control.

They offer words of affirmation, comfort and strength so you know you are not alone when it all feels too much.

Let me walk by your side.

We are in this together.

I have walked this path before. I know a way through.

May I be your guide?

LET GO (I)

She just couldn't let go.
She didn't dare let the feelings in.
Throat tight, heart pounding,
She felt trapped and numb and couldn't breathe.

She was afraid
Of the deep cavern within her.
Bleak and dark,
Terrifying and forbidding.
And she wasn't yet ready
To let herself fall into that place.

She was petrified
That she would never
Land safely
And would spin into free fall
For the rest of her life.

Descending

FEAR OF LETTING GO

The invitation to 'let go' is common in spiritual and wellbeing circles. *Let go of tension... Let go of limiting beliefs...*

Sometimes these invitations bring much relief as they remind us how much we were in fact holding onto. But I've come to realise that it's not always as simple as that. For we may have very good reasons to feel afraid to let go.

Maybe we're in a domestic or work situation where we need to keep our guard up and letting go wouldn't be safe. Maybe there's unprocessed traumatic experiences locked in our body/mind, so our psychological defences are trying to keep us safe by not letting go. In these circumstances we need support and guidance to help us to learn to let go in a way that won't expose us to harm or re-traumatise us.

But perhaps the reason that so many of us find it difficult to let go is because our emotions feel so alien to us. Or we're fearful we'll be overwhelmed if we open that firmly locked door. Or maybe we've just got used to feeling numb. Or we're afraid we won't like what we find because we've been socialised to believe that anger is bad, displaying your emotions means you're irrational, articulating your feelings and desires makes you needy, or being sensitive is weak.

Are there emotions *you* are afraid of feeling? Maybe anger, regret, jealousy, fear, insecurity, loneliness, sorrow, grief? If so, could you at least name them?

How would it be to let go of some of the resistance around allowing in these feelings? What are you afraid will happen? What do you need to feel safer? What small step could you take today or tomorrow (or soon) towards meeting that need?

WHEN DARKNESS CALLS (I)

When darkness calls
It is time
To listen.
To part ways
With your everyday self,
For now.

When darkness calls
It is time
To let go.
To descend
And journey to the underworld
Where your soul awaits.

When darkness calls
It is time
To commit.
To honour
Your deepest self
And your needs and dreams.

When darkness calls
It is time
For courage.
To let yourself die
A thousand deaths.
So you can be
Reborn.

Descending

HEARING THE CALL

Like me, you may have spent many years oblivious to the parts of you that were longing to be seen, to be validated and accepted, to be heard.

Your sadness, your anger, your burning rage. Your self-judgment, your low self-worth, your confusion. Your loneliness, your sorrow, your fatigue.

But you kept going. You tried to keep calm and you carried on, hoping the nagging sensation that something needed attending to would go away. And perhaps, also like me, you wound up exhausted, feeling empty and drained of life.

Until something clicked inside, and you finally realised that you'd expended way too much energy bottling up your feelings and denying your own needs, afraid of what you might find if you let these feelings see the light of day.

And something shifted within you. You decided it was time to try something different. You heard the call. The call to attend to that within you which is longing to be listened to.

And so, I invite you to reflect on these questions – perhaps just quietly in your own mind, or write in a journal:

- What is calling to you for your attention?
- What feelings are challenging you?
- What led you to read this book?
- What do you need?

May you trust and honour that part of you which is courageous enough to attend to your deepest needs.

I AM WITH YOU

May I sit with you?
Feel my presence here, at your side,
So you know that you are not alone.

Let me bear witness to your grief
Let me see your tears
Let me listen to words both voiced and unspoken.

For I too have been in these depths
I too have known despair, hopelessness and desolation
I too have felt invisible, broken and beyond repair
I too have gazed, shadow-eyed, into the abyss
Feeling oblivion calling me.

Yet I am still here.
Can you feel my presence?
Rooted in compassion.
Burning with fierce and tender love.
I am here, beside you
So you need never feel alone.

Descending

THE COMMUNITY OF ALL THINGS

The truth is, even during my darkest times, I realise now that I was never alone. There was always something available to me to offer comfort and solace and companionship. I just needed to remember to look up and see it. And you can, too.

I'm not asking you to avoid or downplay your very real feelings and challenges. I'm inviting you to broaden your perspective, even if just a little, so you may feel how there is more in your life than the difficulties you're currently experiencing.

So, can you notice something now that helps you to feel that you are not alone, here in this moment? Maybe it's the presence of good people nearby or in your life, a photograph of a loved one, the presence or mental image of a pet, or even a favourite flower or tree.

Perhaps it's a sense of being part of a community – of people with similar interests, views or life experience. Whether you know them personally or not, can you sense this community is out there in the wider world and that you are a part of it?

Can you let yourself feel held by the rich tapestry of life? How would it be to soften into the knowledge that all beings on this planet are connected? We all breathe the same air. We are all walking on and nurtured by the same earth beneath us. We are all touched by the same sunlight that streams down from the sky.

And can you sense my presence? I am speaking to you now, across time, through the words on this page.

Dear one, I am with you. You are not alone.

DESCENDING

Breath by breath
Heartbeat by heartbeat
Tear by tear

She descended
Into the cave
Of her soul

To let herself die
And wait for the day
She would be ready
To be reborn.

AN INVITATION

The ability to release our challenging feelings requires us first to summon the courage to feel them and listen to their messages.

Otherwise, and I speak from experience, we will likely get stuck. Stuck in rumination as we chew over the same issues without any resolution. Or stuck in the seeming safety of frozen numbness where we can't feel our pain ... but neither can we feel pleasure, love or joy.

This requires the courage to surrender and descend into the deep emotional waters that you may be fearful to enter.

But there is no rush to enter – you do not need to blindly leap into the underworld waters without support. How would it be to ease yourself in?

To begin this process, I invite you to reflect on this: how would it be to let go of some of the struggle and give yourself over to the courageous act of feeling your feelings and allowing them to move through you?

Can you invoke a feeling of inner strength? Can you summon trust in yourself?

Can you sense how it is, in the end, more painful to deny, resist and struggle with your difficult feelings than to let them in and sit with them?

Remember, it is human to struggle. It is human to feel loss and grief and doubt. It is human to need to feel safe and content and loved.

So please understand, no matter what you are feeling, it is all part of the glorious complexity of being human.

UNRAVELLING

Unravelling.
Unbinding.
Unlearning.
Moving inwards.
Deeper
Towards the tender wounds.
Touching them.
Recoiling.
Then
Softening.
Opening
To their gold.

Descending

UNRAVEL THE THREADS

Now you may find the idea of 'unravelling' somewhat undesirable.

Perhaps you're afraid you'll come apart at the seams.

But maybe you are also drawn to the idea of disentangling the knotted emotional threads within you so you can feel clearer and freer.

If so, I invite you to ponder on what is unravelling within you ... and within your life.

How would it be to begin to unravel these threads – even if just a little – in a way which feels okay for you?

What protective strategies are bound tightly around your tender inner wounds?

Could you begin to peel a layer away in a manner that does not feel overwhelming?

Perhaps you could journal on this.

Begin with the words: *I am unravelling...* and just write whatever comes up for you.

Let it through.

Or simply quietly acknowledge to yourself that you're hurting, and offer this tender bundled-up place within you some compassion and kindness.

SOME DAYS

Some days
The hole in my soul
Feels cavernous
And I am falling, falling
With nothing to hold onto.

Some days
The pain
Feels so intense
That the need to howl
Silences me.

Some days
The deep loneliness
Overwhelms me
And I choose numbness
Because it is easier that way.

Some days
I feel like giving up.

But then.
A flame flickers within my heart…
And a tender warmth spreads
Through my body and soul,

And I know I am not alone.

Descending

BE A FRIEND TO YOURSELF

Some days we get stuck in a rut of a low mood, feeling bad about ourselves.

Self-criticism kicks in and in turn we kick ourselves with the added pain of self-reproach and shame for not being able to feel better, or deal with the challenges, or move on.

We'll often talk to ourselves harshly in a way we would never dream of speaking to a good friend.

So, how about being that good friend to *yourself*?

In learning to cope with grief and loss and all the challenging feelings that come with being human, you will greatly benefit from learning how to be on your own side.

I've found it life changing.

Being on your own side means being kinder to yourself; it means being compassionate and *taking steps to ease your suffering*.

Being on your own side means looking after yourself and standing up for yourself; it includes acknowledging your needs and finding ways of meeting them in a psychologically healthy way.

Being on your own side motivates you to act on your own behalf. It will help you through difficult times.

This is not selfish, nor is it self-indulgent.

And it doesn't mean you're setting yourself against other people.

Life is not a zero-sum game: your being for yourself does not mean you're saying you're not there for others.

And, after all, why shouldn't you be on your side?

Know that it is okay to be on your own side! It's allowed. It's right. It feels good.

Adopt this as a moral principle – a belief to install. It's not going to hurt anyone. And it *is* going to help you.

Decide to be determined about this. Decide to dig deep and bring some grit to this – you're going to come through for yourself.

You've had enough of feeling sad and lonely. You're going to find the courage and determination you need and be a friend to yourself from this point onwards.

So how would it be to offer yourself some warmth and compassion on difficult days?

And in doing so acknowledge your suffering matters – as do your needs, hopes and dreams.

Can you show yourself some tender-hearted concern and be an ally to yourself?

Be kind to yourself.

Soothe yourself.

Whisper to yourself:

'There-there, it hurts I know, but I'm here for you.

This is difficult – but I know I am not alone in my suffering.

May this pain pass; may I find more ease; may I be kind to myself.'

Give yourself a hug.

Stroke your own cheek.

Be gentle and loving.

Mother yourself.

And you also might like to place a hand warmly over your heart and imagine a candle flame within you: the light and warmth of an inner life force that can never be extinguished, even on the darkest of days.

Go gently. It *will* pass.

DEATH MOTHER

When the Death Mother comes
With her poison-tipped barbs
With her voice in your head
Telling you that you are worthless
And bad and to blame…

When the Death Mother comes
With her Gorgon glare
With her shame-filled accusations
Telling you that you are
The cause of others' pain and disappointment...

Remember my presence, my child.
Remember me, the Great Mother,
Who sees you in your entirety,
Who loves all parts of you,
Who knows and upholds
Your essential goodness.

I will never shame you or blame you,
I will never attack you or make you feel wrong,
I will always hold you.
I am holding you now.

Rest in my presence,
Fall into my embrace,
Come home to my love.
And know that you are always welcome here.
For you are always in my heart.

Descending

THE INNER CRITIC

We all have a voice in our head running a commentary on ourselves, our lives and other people.

But this inner voice becomes toxic when it is constantly in critical mode; when all it does is judge what you do or say, replaying situations over and over, shaming you, telling you what you 'should' have said or done.

This inner critic analyses every waking moment and each action you take, telling you that you're not measuring up or you're not doing it right, or you're just a plain old waste of space.

It is spiteful and doesn't hold its punches. It never offers constructive criticism.

It has an uncanny knack of knowing precisely which buttons to press to make you question your worth. It undermines your skills and knowledge. It always knows best. It brooks no argument. It is dismissive and mean.

It can reduce you to a quivering state of self-loathing and it may feel utterly futile to try and counter its withering, destructive energy.

It is punishing you for being who you are and acting like you do. And as you've likely been told you're too sensitive at some point in your life, then the inner critic is attacking you for that too, even though it's how you're wired and cannot be changed.

Sound familiar?

Perhaps we can lessen its sting somewhat by renaming it the 'itty bitty shitty committee'.

Another name for this punishing inner critic is the *Critical Parent*, and in its extreme form, the *Death Mother*.

The archetypal *Death Mother* can be seen as harmful and traumatising energy which comes to us from a person, institution, culture, or nation state that we would naturally expect to nurture, protect and support us, and exists not only in the outer world but also in the inner world of our own minds and bodies and leads us to bring harmful and traumatising energy to ourselves[5].

Now, if you've received parenting from someone who was, or still is, critical and/or shaming and knows how to press your buttons, well, that inner voice has plenty of ammunition and an immense playbook from which to draw doesn't it?

In contrast, the *Great Mother* can be seen as the energy of unconditional love, support and nurturing – she who provides and sustains; she who is compassionate, open, welcoming and generous.

The Great Mother can be considered both an external spiritual presence – such as Mother Earth or the Goddess or mother-figures in religions such as Mary in Christianity – as well as an internal energy within our own minds and bodies.

So, how would it be to rest in the loving arms of the Great Mother, however this concept may resonate with you?

Her love is unconditional. She will never judge or attack you.

---

[5] Daniela F. Sieff 'A Brief Introduction to the Archetypal Death Mother', see: danielasieff.com/the-archetypal-death-mother

If you can sense this presence, try to internalise it – notice where and how you feel this loving presence in your body. Sink into it. And let the feeling sink into you.

Or if 'Great Mother' as a term doesn't work for you, replace this with the name of a figure or energy that generates feelings of being safe, protected and at peace.

And call upon this figure or energy whenever you feel an attack of the Death Mother coming on.

STONE

I am like stone.
Heart heavy
Trapped
Beneath a boulder
Of grief.

I am like stone.
Stuck within
An immoveable
Rockface
Of sadness.

I am like stone.
Still, silent
Watching
The world
Through numbness.

But just like the stone
Has its own soul
And way of being,
This is the form
I must currently take,
The home I must inhabit.

And, just like the stone
I too am strong
And present,
Ancient and wise

Holding millions of years
Within my body.

So, for now, I will be like stone
And allow the healing waters
Of my tears
To smooth the rough edges
And let the force
Of my grief
Crack me open
To reveal
The seam of jewels
Within.

BEING WITH WHAT IS

In difficult times you may wish you felt differently; you may yearn for better days; you may feel frustrated and irritated that you can't seem to move on.

So often we add to our original difficulties and create additional inner tension by trying to push away the strong feelings, painful emotions, or troublesome thoughts.

Buddhist teachings talk of the *Two Arrows*.

The first arrow that hits us is the pain of the original thought, emotion or experience.

Then we hit ourselves with a second – even more painful – arrow (and a third, fourth and fifth…) when we reject how we're feeling and create stories around how things should or should not be.

There is much wisdom in being with what is.

You don't have to like it.

And you certainly don't have to stay in that place forever.

But by letting go of resistance to your current emotional state or thoughts you may find an unexpected ease arises that enables you to open to the healing power of kindness and self-compassion.

And you may find that this, in turn, allows you to tap into intuitive insight and guidance around what you need and what steps to take next.

So, I invite you to reflect: what is the form that you must take at this point in your life?

Do *you* too feel like stone?

Or perhaps you feel airy and boundaryless, or perhaps numb and foggy.

Perhaps you feel like a tumultuous ocean, or you're burning like an out-of-control wildfire.

What are the words you would use?

And how would it be to inhabit this form? What is it saying to you? What does it need from you? What wisdom is it whispering to you?

GRIEF MOVES

May you allow yourself to grieve.
To truly feel your losses
And sense grief's whispers in your body.

May you learn to listen with compassion
As grief reveals its messages
Through images, sensations and colours.

May you feel how grief moves
When you heed it.
It shifts and changes,
It flares and fades.

May you find the courage
To open to your grief
Deeply and fully
So that it may move through you.

And, as grief moves,
May you feel
How it is creating
Space within you
To let life in again

So you may open your heart
To joy.

Descending

HOW TO FEEL

I've spoken about feeling your feelings. But, practically, how do you do that?

Well, it's as simple – and challenging – as taking moments to be mindfully aware of the sensations in your body, the tone of your emotional landscape and the contents of your thoughts.

To feel your grief, heartache and sorrow or your anger, frustration and confusion, you need to sit with them, notice and listen.

It's an act of paying attention.

Notice how and where you feel the emotion in your body – perhaps it's a lump in your throat, a heaviness in the pelvis, a pressure in the chest... And ask it what it has to say... What it needs... And be kind to yourself by trying to do what you can to meet those needs.

It's as simple and radical – and challenging – as that.

But it is not a one-off act. It is a vital regular practice.

Try it, and you will very likely sense a shift in your inner landscape.

A spontaneous tenderness may arise within you. A softening. A release of tension. A warm-hearted compassion for your suffering.

You may touch the grief that is at the heart of your sorrow. And perhaps healing tears will begin gently to flow.

Let grief move you and move through you. This is the path to healing.

HEALING WATERS

May your tears
Flow
Into the great river
Of life
And may you feel
Held
By these sacred waters
As they carry you
Home.

Descending

THE HEALING POWER OF TEARS

It is often said that tears are healing waters.

How would it be to let your tears flow?

There is no shame in crying. It isn't childish. Tears do not signify a lack of control. They are not a sign of weakness or fragility. You're not being over-emotional or too sensitive.

To cry when you feel sad or angry brings release – and relief. It is part of the way we humans express ourselves.

Perhaps your tears are words that cannot find expression. But they need to come out somehow.

I know from experience that swallowing down tears and trying to ignore them creates further pain.

A lump in the throat.

A heavy heart.

A soul crying out to be heard.

Perhaps you can feel them too – your unexpressed tears?

Where is their energy lodged in *your* body?

And I also know that when I give myself permission and space to cry, whether a tender little sniffle of sadness or a howling gale of grief, I always feel brighter and clearer afterwards.

So how would it be to honour *your* tears?

And to let yourself cry as a sacred act of honouring all parts of yourself?

A QUESTION

Whose life have you been living?
Because if it's not your own
Then you're living a lie.

Descending

LIVING YOUR OWN LIFE

Have you ever felt the niggling sense that there's something out of kilter in your life? That something doesn't quite feel right? That you're not living the life you're meant to? That you're not living *your* life?

There are numerous reasons why this might be so.

You may have chosen a career path earlier in life to fulfil the expectations of parents. You may have been limited by socio-economic or cultural factors which frustrated your attempts to follow your dreams or outright excluded you. You may have made choices that were not in your best interests that impacted your life's trajectory so far. You may have got so used to prioritising other people's needs, comfort and expectations that you forgot how to please yourself.

If this resonates then I invite you to reflect on what feels out of kilter in your life… And on what needs changing to bring it back into alignment.

I recognise that some issues may seem too huge to change, but I'm also a believer that frequent small steps can lead to more profound change over time.

And so, I also invite you to consider: what small steps could you take today, and over the coming days, to realign your life so that it feels more congruent with your values, needs and dreams?

Listen to the wise whispers of your soul and then take a simple baby step. And remember that one step leads to another, and then one day, you will look back and see how far you've come.

BRUISED

If your life is too small
For the infinite complex beauty that is your soul
Then you'll keep bumping into yourself
Until, covered in bruises of painful yearning,
One day you will wake up
And realise you must find a way
To escape and be free.

SOUL WHISPERS

Do you understand this? You are a unique expression of life living itself.

There is no-one, there never has been, and never will be anyone else with your unique combination of talents, values, experience and perspectives.

You were born with a gift to share with the world to contribute to the rich tapestry of life for the betterment of humanity and all living things, as well as for your own satisfaction, authenticity and joy.

Yet too many of us live as if this were not the case.

Our materialistic culture encourages us to live our lives as if they had no true meaning, other than chasing the dopamine hit of our next purchase. And we may feel trapped by circumstances, expectations, habits and beliefs.

It hurts to live in such a soul-denying way.

Yet still the soul has its agenda. The soul will not be ignored.

It speaks through images and sensations. It speaks through interests and themes that recur through your life. It speaks through insistent longings. It speaks through grief, sorrow and pain.

It urges you to live a meaningful life.

Our soul speaks to each of us daily, if we could but slow down and listen.

Have you heard the call of your soul yet?

ASHES

Her anger
Consumed her
With shame.
She was reduced
To a pile of grey ashes
Scattered
By the fickle winds
Of worrying
About what other people
Might think.

Descending

HONOURING ANGER

Anger is an emotion with a bad reputation: many of us are afraid of it and strive to deny and stifle our angry feelings.

Yet anger is an important, valid and healthy emotion: it is a sign that a boundary has been crossed.

You're likely to experience anger if you feel attacked, deceived, frustrated, invalidated or unfairly treated.

Feeling angry about something can be useful because it can:

- help us identify problems or things that are hurting us;
- motivate us to create change, achieve our goals and move on; and
- help us stay safe and defend ourselves in dangerous situations by giving us a burst of energy as part of our fight or flight system.[6]

It's an emotion whose energy, when experienced cleanly and channelled effectively, can be used.

Harnessed, you can channel its energy outwards to fuel direct action and effect change from a place of rooted presence.

And yet that's not the common experience of anger, is it? Too often we deny it, stifle it and damp it down.

---

[6] mind.org.uk/information-support/types-of-mental-health-problems/anger/about-anger

If you experience conflict about your anger, may I suggest you consider this?

How would it be to realise that by denying your anger you are ignoring a red flashing light that is warning you that something is wrong?

Can you understand that by ignoring anger you are perpetuating the cycle of neglecting your own needs which you were taught by an unhealthy culture that disregards emotions – and especially women's anger?

Now, it's not helpful to stay stuck in anger, particularly if it's self-pitying and impotent and stops you moving forward. That said, you may well feel self-pity when you realise how much you have to be angry at, and that's fine, but you don't want to get trapped there.

We're aiming for your anger to burn 'clean' i.e. an anger that empowers you to be on your own side, stand up for yourself and set and uphold healthy boundaries.

And this starts with admitting to yourself that you're feeling angry, noticing where you feel it in your body and engaging with its messages by asking: what does it need?

So, I invite you to reflect on these questions if you wish to acknowledge and work with your angry feelings:

- How do you experience anger?
- Where do you feel it in your body?
- What's your relationship with it?
- Are you scared of it? Ashamed of it? Do you damp it down?
- Can you create a safe space to be with it, and to ask it what it has to tell you and what it needs?

Let's reappraise anger as a helpful and healthy emotion because its simple and important message is that a boundary has been crossed.

Own your anger – it has much wisdom to teach you.

Let it burn brightly so instead of being reduced to ashes by shame, you become a phoenix, rising in glory!

UNBOUND

Life is a sacred journey,
Unfolding moon by moon.
And as you unfold,
Breath by breath
Expand into the space
Created by uncreasing
The hardened corners,
And disentangling
The knotted threads
Of your needs and desires.
Unwinding, unbinding
Your deepest longings
As you slowly unfurl
And answer the yearning
To surrender
And be held
By the flow of life.

Descending

UNWINDING

When you're in the grip of anxiety or anger, of sadness or frustration you will likely get physically tense – your thoughts creating tension in your body; the physical tension feeding the spiral of racing thoughts or heavy feelings.

Taking a conscious breath or two can help you to unwind, even if just a little, because breathing directly impacts your nervous system. When you breathe in, oxygen surges into your brain, the sympathetic branch of your nervous system is activated, and your heartbeat naturally increases. Breathing out activates the parasympathetic branch of your nervous system which soothes your body and mind and the heart beats more slowly. Each inhale brings life and energy, each exhale offers the invitation to soften and slow down.

If it feels safe and good for you, try this simple exercise:

First just notice where you feel the breath in your body … perhaps it's the flow of air over your upper lip, or the sensation of air in the nostrils… Perhaps it's the rise and fall of your chest and/or abdomen. Just gently notice…

Now, can you notice that with each out-breath your body physically relaxes? Perhaps there's a softening in the face – the eyes, the jaw, and maybe your shoulders drop a little… Perhaps there's a sensation of release in the belly … in your hands… Perhaps you notice your feet on the ground now…

Let the in-breath take care of itself. Just gently and softly rest your awareness on your out-breath… Soften into the pause at the end of each exhalation, for a few more rounds…

You can do this. You can be held by the sacred ever-unfolding flow of life.

PORTAL

May your grief
Be the portal
Through which
You courageously step
To begin
The longed-for journey
Home to your soul.

GRIEF AS A PORTAL

I have found that when I consciously engage with my feelings of grief and sorrow and offer myself heartfelt compassion, it's as if I enter an altered state of consciousness.

It's as if I slip beyond the veil that usually obscures this depth of feeling.

It's as if I step through a portal into a place where I feel held and unconditionally loved.

Sometimes I feel myself floating in a sky full of stars, held by the invisible yet tangibly loving presence of the divine.

It's a place where true healing happens. A place from which I will return to my daily life with a gift to bring with me.

Each time I enter this space I am strengthening the sense of being held in the arms of our common humanity.

Each time I sink into this ocean of kindness I am reminding myself of my essential goodness and that my true nature is to love and be loved.

And as I let that remembrance sink into me it becomes more and more natural to live from that embodied knowledge in my daily life.

I believe that our most profound and intense feelings can act as sacred portals that help us move beyond our everyday consciousness and into the presence of our soul.

And in this soul space we may open to wise insight and receive guidance from that part of us which knows what we need and loves us beyond words.

THE SCAR

You have walked too long
With this pain
To refuse its beckoning now.

So turn towards it
And let its searing
Tear your heart.

Bleeding.
Opened.
A tender presence
Comforts you.

As you feel,
As if for the first time,
Held.
And maybe even whole.

The balm
Of love
Knits together
The wound.

And the scar
Shall remind you:
You are never alone.

Descending

TENDING YOUR WOUNDS

There comes a time in your life when your long-buried wounds rise to the surface and burst open, and you have no choice but to tend to them.

Those wounds you've spent your life looking away from, pushing them down into the underworld of your psyche as a way of protecting yourself from the pain.

Until one day, you can ignore them no longer.

And when this happens – when the pain beckons – perhaps it is because now you are ready.

Ready, at last, to offer yourself the compassion, to take the grounded action and to reach out for the support that you need.

Ready at last, to heal.

Though perhaps, just as a wound to your flesh may leave a scar behind, healing the wounds to your soul will leave its own mark.

A tenderness. Subtle yet sensitive.

A memento of the journey taken, and the inner work done.

A reminder that what you experienced is now in the past.

May you courageously heed you soul's beckoning so that one day you will cherish your tender emotional scars as a reminder of your capacity for healing.

And may they also remind you of the loving presence of support within and all around you: a presence that is holding you now.

A BLESSING FROM THE DEPTHS

May you find the courage to sink beneath the surface.
May you learn to see in the dark.
May you unearth the gifts buried within your pain.
May you discover answers in the void.
And through it all may you feel held
By the warm embrace of limitless self-compassion and kindness.

IN THE WINTRY UNDERWORLD

I speak to you from the heart of darkness.

That place where it feels like all the lights have gone out. Where nothing makes sense anymore. Where the past is tainted with sadness and the future seems unthinkable.

After a good while struggling, resisting, pretending all was okay, I have surrendered to this place – for it is where it seems I need to be.

The descent was messy and left me bruised.

But then I landed.

I landed in that place I had most feared and resisted.

And though it is a place that can feel lonely and isolating – as the muffled sounds of life continuing on the surface seem so far away – there is a curious comfort in finally allowing myself to be here.

This cave of not-knowing. The underworld.

And as I close my eyes and give myself to the darkness, I can hear-feel a sound. A throb.

Da-dum. Da-dum. A heartbeat… My heartbeat…? No, it is the pulse of life, throbbing in the darkness. A reminder that while part of me may have died, this is not the end.

Da-dum. Da-dum. And I realise… I am in the underworld tomb-womb of the Great Mother. And I am not alone.

Da-dum. Da-dum. And I know I must close my eyes and listen. I must allow myself to feel. All of it.

I am safe here. For She is holding me – the Great Mother who will cradle me in this wintry death-like place until I am ready to return.

Here I am sharing with you poems and reflections that offer validation for your pain and gently guide you to find meaning in your sorrow so you can feel that you aren't struggling in vain.

Here you will find pieces that invite you to pause and reflect on the nature of your feelings. They ask you to delve a little deeper so you can gain greater self-understanding and acceptance.

And they invite you to shift your perspective so you might discover seams of tender and fierce self-compassion as the soul-shaking tremors of the descent begin to subside.

Can you let yourself be here in the wintry underworld, if and when you need to be?

Can you close your eyes and hear the beating heart of Life?

And can you let yourself be held by the Great Mother and surrender to what needs to be felt… To be acknowledged… To be honoured and revered?

For this is the place where healing happens. This is the place where you can lay down the burdens you have carried for too long. This is the sanctuary into which you can crawl and release the struggle. This is the soul forge of the underworld. And here you will be remoulded and then reborn.

It is time to land now, and rest awhile in this wintry place. May I guide you?

WHEN DARKNESS CALLS (II)

When darkness calls
Light a candle
So that you may make the darkness visible,
So you may turn to face your shadow,
So you may discover the gold in the depths.

When darkness calls
Light a candle
That is the light
In your heart
Bathing all parts of you
With love.

When darkness calls
Light a candle
That may slowly illumine
The complexity
And sacred splendour
Of your soul.

THE GIFTS OF DARKNESS

When I speak of bringing light to the inner darkness, I am not speaking of bypassing your challenges or pain with false positivity; I am not speaking of choosing love over fear; nor am I speaking of prioritising the light over the dark.

Far from it. This light I speak of is not a false bravura designed to chase away the demons.

I speak of *making the darkness visible* NOT of lighting up the darkness.

This is a subtle but essential distinction.

So much of our inner turmoil, reactivity and pain arises from past woundings that remain unseen, uncared for, shamed, belittled, pushed down, rejected.

These parts of us do not need further rejection through bypassing them with fake positivity. These vulnerable and wounded parts require gentle coaxing.

They need us to build inner resources of self-worth and self-compassion. They long for our love.

So let your inner candle be the gentle focus of your kind attention.

May it illuminate your hidden parts so that they feel safe enough to reveal themselves – both the gold of your gifts and the shadows of your rejected traits – so you might begin to know them.

So you might learn to love all that you are.

WASTELAND

Parched. Bereft. Hopeless.
Cracked. Crumbling. Dry.
This wasteland
Is a lifeless place.
A void of longing, confusion and doubt.

And yet I know
That being here
Is a necessary step
On the journey to wholeness.
A space to be navigated
That I now must call home.

And so I surrender to the bone-dry land,
Close my eyes and trust
Until I see the truth
That only I can revivify this parched earth of my heart.

So breath by breath
And step by step
I water the arid soil of my numbness
With hope and trust and tiny joys.

And I hold the vision
That, when it is ready,
A new green tendril of life
Will break through.

YOUR INNER LANDSCAPE

The metaphor of the 'wasteland' representing something that is spiritually and emotionally arid and unsatisfying is one that speaks to the soul, I feel.

It's a powerful image of neglect and abandonment, used famously by the poet T.S. Eliot to represent the spiritual and intellectual decay of the modern world.

His poem was written in 1922, but there's an anonymous 13th century French poem called *The Elucidation* that uses this metaphor too.

This earlier poem recounts the story of a place long ago where well maidens were the guardian spirits of the land and would appear and serve food and drink to weary travellers.

That is, until one day when the avaricious and lustful king raped a well maiden and stole her sacred chalice. And hearing of what he had done, across the country men raped and stole from the well maidens too.

Now the maidens no longer came from their wells, and they no longer offered their abundance and waters.

And so, because of this crime the once moist and fertile land became arid and devoid of life and all goodness withered and died: it became a barren wasteland.

*

As well as being a startling metaphor that speaks to the conditions mankind has created through plundering the Earth of her resources, this story is also symbolic of how we may treat ourselves.

A wasteland is barren in soul. It has been taken for granted, mistreated, plundered until all that is creative and kind withers and dies.

Our hustle and grind culture encourages and rewards us for doing this to ourselves.

To keep going when we need to rest.

To compete when our soul would be better fed by collaboration.

To strive for the illusory comforts of materialism when our heart knows they are empty of meaning and will leave us feeling starved of purpose and true satisfaction.

When we blindly follow this paradigm or feel unavoidably coerced into following it, we are violating our own souls and stealing from our dreams and in doing so we deplete our life force to the extent that our inner landscape may become barren and devoid of life, hope and joy.

It feels like recognising this and taking steps to tend to our inner landscape with kindness and sincere care is essential work: vital for self-understanding and healing.

So may we each of us tend the wasteland in our hearts and souls so that we both resuscitate our self-respect and resurrect respect for the miracle of life itself.

May we find our way back to our wild and instinctual nature and may we tend to the longings of our soul.

May we lovingly accept the deep waters of our emotions so that we might feel again and tap into a powerful wellspring of compassion for ourselves, each other, and our planet – our home.

And may we remember that we live in a vast ocean of connection and harm done to one is harm done to us all.

*

Does the concept of an inner wasteland resonate with you?

If so, reflect on these questions:

- What does this wasteland look like?
- How does it feel?
- What does it need?
- How could you tend its parched soil?
- What tiny joys could you water it with?
- What hope might you cultivate?
- And do you have a sense of what the new green tendril of life returning would symbolise for you?

LIMINAL

Between the worlds
Of who you were
And who you're meant to be

Blinded by confusion
There's no way out
That you can see.

You wander
In the darkness of this place
Between past
And possibility

But if you can surrender
To this void
And trust,
Then you'll find yourself
And you'll be free.

UNANSWERED QUESTIONS

Sometimes not knowing is the answer to your question.

Sometimes there's nothing you can do but sit with this not knowing, no matter how frustrating it is, no matter how strongly you yearn for clarity.

Sometimes you might need to be in this space for days, months … even years.

This liminal space of not knowing is a threshold between what has passed and what is yet to come.

You are being held in a chrysalis.

Your old form is dissolving.

Your new shape is yet to develop.

This cannot be rushed.

It has its own sacred timing.

Your task here is to dig deep for strength and to call forth the patience to hold this tension … and trust that all is coming and that, when it does, it will be beautiful to behold.

I DON'T KNOW

I don't know who I am any more.
My body is changing,
My face is ageing,
My steps feel uncertain.

I don't know who I am any more.
All the old identities
And labels I'd worked for
Are falling away.

I don't know who I am any more.
My inner world
Is spinning
And I can't make it stop.

I don't know who I am any more.
The leaves on the tree
That was once in full bloom
Are changing colour, getting ready to drop.

Yet, perhaps this not knowing
Is a gift
In disguise.
A clue
From the other side.

Maybe this not knowing
Is a chance
To stop

Breathe, and pause.

What if this not knowing
Is an invitation
To become
Who I was always meant to be?

So yes, I don't know who I am any more.
What a delicious
Opportunity
To decide
To be me.

NOT KNOWING

There are many times in our lives when we just don't know what to do next.

When we are in the underworld of a dark night of the soul when it feels like we're disintegrating and we feel utterly discombobulated and confused, I think all we can truly 'do' is to surrender and to let go into not knowing.

It's not easy.

But it is necessary.

I wrote the above poem deep in the 'not knowing' of midlife; a time when old identities can fall away. A time between the passing of youth and the coming of the third age. A time when your soul demands that you reappraise your life and decide who you truly want to be.

I'd been struggling and struggling ... and then, as these words came to me, I felt an inner shift.

A call to surrender to the process.

To let it do its work on me.

Instead of struggling to hold on to who I thought I was, I saw that this tussle was an opportunity to drop all the masks and expectations, to stop bowing at the altar of what other people think, to no longer look outside myself for guidance, and sink deeply into the person I want to be.

My authentic self.

Fully and freely expressed.

What a delicious opportunity indeed!

So, might your struggles with parts of yourself or your life be an opportunity to release an old version of you?

How is this period in your life asking you to decide to be YOU?

VERNALIZATION

Spring has come
And yet I still feel
Dead inside.
As if the warm golden light
Is mocking
The barren wasteland of my heart.

Yet a part of me knows
That I must experience
The numbing chill
Of this inner winter
A while longer.

I must allow myself
To receive the full force
Of winter's death
So that vernalization can occur.

And so I choose to trust
That this desolate inner winter
Is part of the healing process.

And that feeling the full force
Of the frozen grief and sadness
Will enable me
To bloom and blossom
Once again.

EMOTIONAL SEASONS

We all move through the seasons in the inner landscapes of our thoughts, emotions and spiritual connection.

We have spring-like seasons of hopefulness, curiosity and inspiration. We experience summery joy, sensuality and radiance. Other times we enter autumnal phases of heightened sensitivity, intuition and discernment. And then there are the inner winter times where we're in a death-like dark void of frozen stillness. But this also holds the potential for clarity, healing and renewal.

This inner journey may correspond with the seasons of the year, but external events can suddenly plunge you into a barren frozen winter, or perhaps you find yourself descending through autumn into winter for no apparent reason, or maybe you've felt stuck in winter for a long time, and you wonder if spring will ever come.

I invite you to reflect on which season you're currently in, emotionally. And no matter where you are, how would it be to acknowledge that life moves in cycles and that this state will not last forever?

Can you let yourself be held by the potent rhythm of the sacred cycle of life – that of birth, growth, release, death and renewal? Can you sense how you embody the truth that all of life is change?

*

(By the way, *vernalization* is the process by which plants use a prolonged cold period to promote flowering. This fallow time is essential for their survival and ability to thrive.)

WINTERING

In the harsh bleakness of winter
May you remember
That your roots are nourished
By this fertile darkness
That your heart is held safe
In the cocoon of stillness
That your confusion is dispelled
By the frost-cold winds.
May you embrace this inner winter
Wrapped up cosily by the fireside of your soul
And embrace the opportunity
To rest and be renewed.

INNER WINTERS

Let's take a moment to reflect on the season of winter.

Winter is the darkest point of the year. It can feel bleak and hopeless. The branches are bare. Cold air makes your teeth chatter and takes the breath away. Grey skies seem featureless and uninviting.

Yet while all seems barren above ground, deep in the soil seeds and plant roots are developing and growing, feeding the plant until warmer weather returns, ready to revivify and flourish when spring arrives.

Winter is a space between worlds. It's the centre of the spiral of life. The end of the out-breath of the year where all is silent and still … before the inhale of spring comes, bringing rebirth, potential and new possibilities.

How would it be to reconsider difficult periods in your life as inner winters?

Just as seasonal winter is essential for plants and trees to rest and renew so they can grow again, if you can honour your own inner winters – those times of loss or low mood or other challenging feelings – then perhaps you too can let the mystery of life work through you; perhaps you can find the courage metaphorically to let die what needs to die; let the part of your life or identity that needs to leave, go; dig deep roots into the ground of courage; and metabolise the pain.

In our inner winters we may appear quiet and down. We may withdraw from the outside world, even from friends and loved ones. We may no longer find enjoyment in activities we used to. We separate from the world and go inwards.

But these inner winters can be a time of transformation too. They invite you to tend to your interior landscape; to dive deep into your psyche so you can understand yourself better and heal from past experiences and hurts.

Inner winters invite you to quieten your outer life so you can focus your energy inwards and spend time with yourself, listening to what needs to be heard.

How would it be to welcome an inner winter as an opportunity to nurture what is calling to be brought forth next in your life?

But don't rush now. Allow yourself to pause... This is a process that needs space and time to unfold. It asks for self-compassion and patience. You are suspended in the fertile void, that space between death and rebirth. Time has stopped. Past, present and future co-exist.

It is not linear or logical. It has its own sacred timing that you cannot consciously control or rush. In these depths, let all else drop away. In this space all is possible. This place has the capacity to offer renewal and rejuvenation. It offers opportunity for deep healing and personal growth.

But you will likely find this challenging.

Try to be kind to yourself if you find you'd rather reach for distractions than be with yourself. Go slowly. Tend to your needs, wants and desires. Comfort yourself with a hug. Treat yourself like a precious object... And know that you are certainly not alone in finding this difficult.

You may feel like you're going around in circles. Especially if you're dealing with emotional wounds from the past; you may find that you cannot believe something has come up again.

Remember that life is cyclic and while it seems as if you're going around in circles you're actually moving in spirals – in and out, in and out. Each spiral is a journey of descent and return. And each spiral is subtly different.

On one spiral down into the depths of your pain you learn a lesson which you bring out to the surface of your life, on the next spiral down you release something and return a little bit lighter and renewed.

There is a mystery to being in an inner winter – it asks you to surrender to the darkness and be held in the void and to open to your soul's whispers…

I believe that when an inner winter calls and we are pulled down into the underworld it is because our soul can no longer let us ignore what is needing to be felt, asking to be processed or yearning to be expressed.

And all in good time you will rise, stronger from your experience, nourished by what you have learned, ready to return to the next springtime of your life. Clearer and wiser.

So I invite you, when you're in the wintry underworld, to consider:

- What is falling away within you and your life?
- What are you ready to release and let die?
- What seeds of new life are buried deep within, asking to be nurtured?

May you receive the blessings of your inner winter: may you find the courage to release that which is ready to die and may you heed the wise whispers of your soul.

REST IN ME

I am always here,
You can rest in me.
Place one hand on your heart
And one on your belly,
And breathe.

Rest in me.
The earth of your body.
Feel my stability and solidity
Be present with my realness
The pulse that throbs
The breath that flows
The strength in my bones
The power in my muscles.

You can rest in me.
I have been with you all your life.
Your memories are in my cells,
Your joys are in my movements
Your laughter lights up my soul
Your tears bring healing.

I know you.
I love you.
You can rest in me.

YOUR BODY AS REFUGE

A refuge is anything that brings you a sense of safety or shelter or a place of sanctuary that offers respite, renewal even perhaps a sense of the sacred.

So, how would it be to consider your own body as the ultimate refuge? A resting place. Your home during this life.

Now, I absolutely acknowledge that this may feel intensely challenging if you're living with physical pain or disabilities. But even when you're experiencing pain or discomfort it's beneficial to realise that if you're alive then you are, on a fundamental level, basically okay.

Your heart is still beating. You are breathing and there is enough air. Your internal organs and systems are performing the billions of processes *every second* necessary to keep you alive. There is refuge in your 'ongoingness' – you're still here. And of course, in a very real sense, your body is ever-present throughout this life. No physical body, no you!

Yes, we humans need protection around us in our external environment, the sanctuary of loving relationships, connections that sustain us and things that bring us joy. But in difficult times it can be helpful to consider your body as your sanctuary. A place to call home.

Here's a simple practice to centre yourself in your physical body, when your emotional world feels difficult:

Place one hand on your heart and one on your belly … and breathe… Feel the energy of life flowing through you… Feel the energy of *your* life flowing through you… You have always been there for yourself – can you see it now?

LET ME ASSURE YOU

You are not bad, my love
For saying 'no more'
To someone who has hurt you
For too long.

You are not self-centred or indulgent
For giving yourself
The space you need
To grieve and heal.

You are not selfish
For putting yourself first at last,
And attending to your needs
And nurturing your desires.

Let me assure you:
This is what you need
This is what you deserve
To find yourself again
And to love all parts of you
Back to life.

BOUNDARIES

Boundaries. One word. A whole world of challenges, particularly for us women who are socialised to be emotional caretakers of others. And especially when the person crossing our boundaries is a parent or loved one.

But you do not have to accept bad behaviour from those around you. You do not have to suffer in silence. You do not have to prioritise their comfort over your mental health. You do not have to ask permission to attend to your own needs.

I have learned this the hard way! After years of trying not to rock the boat in my family and of biting my tongue I felt suffocated, unable to speak my truth. Until I said, 'no more'.

An essential step in the journey out of the underworld is to identify the boundaries of what you will and will not accept from the behaviour of others, and to practise enacting them.

Reflect on these questions, perhaps with your journal:

- What are my boundaries?
- What will I no longer put up with?
- How will I maintain those boundaries?

Here are some useful phrases to keep in mind if someone is gaslighting you by denying your experience is real:

- *I know my truth and I'm not debating it with you.*
- *I hear what you're saying but that was not my experience.*
- *We remember things differently.*
- *My feelings are my feelings, and this is how I feel.*
- *I realise you see things differently, but this is how I see it.*
- *I'm stepping away from this conversation.*

SHE WHISPERS

You too need to be held, my love.
To be seen.
To be heard.
To be mothered.

I will hold you.
I will see you and I will hear you.
I know your magic and your power.

So come home to Me, the Mother Divine.
I am in your heart.
My arms are open and waiting for you…

To hold you.

To welcome you home.

ON FEELING HELD

I think that each of us humans has a fundamental set of needs.

And they are: to feel held; to feel wanted and valued; to feel safe; to feel seen; and to feel loved.

I wonder if these needs are at the root of all our longings.

I wonder whether all our searching, all our efforts to feel complete, and all our erratic and needy behaviours could be satiated by feeling held and safe again, perhaps as we did in our mother's womb.

And this is especially vital for those of us who grew up without being able to develop a secure attachment (i.e. emotional bond) to our parents or carers – this is reckoned to be about 50% of the population.

For us, this need to be safe, loved, valued and seen can feel like a searingly intense search for home.

And then maybe, at a spiritual level, we have a deep yearning to be reunited with the cosmos, with God or Goddess, with the Oneness.

Perhaps we long to feel part of the unity from which we came...

Whatever the motivation, there is something powerfully therapeutic about feeling held – it's as if your entire nervous system relaxes and you finally feel safe.

Yes, being physically held by a loved one may achieve this.

But there's a deeper level of holding that perhaps we also yearn for: that of being held by a force greater than ourselves.

A spiritual holding that is unconditional and will never leave us.

If this calls to you then try this soulful practice. You might like to make a recording of yourself reading this, leaving spacious pauses between each step:

Sit comfortably or maybe even lie down if you prefer…

Feel into the bed, floor or chair beneath you… And let yourself be held…

Scan through your body from head to toe and invite each area to release, to soften…

Your jaw, your eyes, your forehead, the back of your head… Softening, releasing…

Your neck, your shoulders, your arms and hands… Any tension melting away…

Your back… Your chest… Your belly… Releasing, relaxing…

Your hips and pelvis… Your legs … and your feet… Softening, releasing, relaxing…

Breathe out and enjoy the sensation of the release of physical tension and the feeling of relaxation that each out-breath can bring…

Sense the earth beneath you… Strong, stable, nurturing… Holding you… There's nothing else you need to do…

Just rest ... and be held by the loving presence of Mother Earth...

You might gently call to your mind's eye a figure holding you now ... someone or something that represents nurture and safety to you... And they gaze into your eyes with unconditional love...

Breathe... And receive this holding and love...

And let any feelings of safety and the sense of being held sink into every cell of your being ... as you sink into the felt sense of being held.

You are safe here.

You can relax.

LET GO (II)

This time she decided to let go.
Falling, falling, falling
She stopped reaching out for something to hold on to
Or to distract herself or to find something with which to numb out.
So downwards, deeper, darker
She fell.
But this time, in no longer resisting,
She felt herself floating
Supported by an invisible presence
That would keep her safe from harm.
A loving current
That she knew would slow and soften her landing.
And so this time she let go
And she let herself fall
Into the once-terrifying darkness
And discovered
She was no longer alone.

LETTING YOURSELF LET GO

If you've tried to connect to the parts of your inner landscape that feel constricted and fearful, and have tried to help yourself feel safe enough to listen to them, I wonder if you've noticed a shift? Perhaps even a willingness to trust in this process of surrendering to your feelings?

To surrender to our emotional world requires faith in ourselves to be able to process what we find there without being overwhelmed or undone by it.

It's likely that, like me, you've developed behavioural and psychological protections over the years; inner guardians who prevent you from being overwhelmed by difficult feelings and serve to protect the wounded inner child parts of you who feel vulnerable and scared.

You may check out and become foggy and unfocused when you try to sit with your challenging feelings; you may reach for social media or TV to distract yourself; you might get irritable and criticise people around you as a means of distracting yourself from your inner world; or you might use food or drink to self-soothe.

To sit with your feelings you need to feel safe.

One way I've learned to create a sense of inner safety is to ask myself what I need to feel secure enough to get in touch with my anger or sorrow.

Personally, I need to invoke a sense of inner strength and rooted presence and to remind myself of the protections around me.

So I think of times when I *have* felt strong and present.

And I remind myself that I'm safe here where I'm sitting with locked doors, strong walls around me and the solid ground beneath me.

I invoke feelings of safety, strength and presence in my mind and body and marinate in the sensations – let them sink into me as I sink into them.

Then when I feel strong and present, I know I am better resourced to release the protections that are preventing me from entering deeper into my psyche and getting closer to the roots of my anger or grief.

I've also created an 'inner wisdom committee' of guides, and an 'inner soul sanctuary' in my mind's eye – a safe place where I am surrounded by figures who love and see and understand me, and of whom I can request wise guidance.

My soul sanctuary is a cosy room, with deep red walls lined with bookshelves, soft comfortable furniture and a roaring fire in the hearth. I sit down, my inner wisdom committee surrounds me, and I feel safe.

The committee comprises: a strong and athletic warrior-woman who I know would go into battle for me and fight to the death; a mother who looks into my eyes with unconditional love and whispers words of affection and affirmation; a queenly figure who radiates presence and authority and who sets and enforces healthy boundaries for me; and an elder woman – the Silver Lady – who is filled with the wisdom of the world and much insight and I trust her to give me the guidance that I need.

All of this helps me to surrender.

All of this helps me to feel less alone and to trust that I will land in the place that I need to once I let go of the struggle that comes with resisting what is.

What would your soul sanctuary look like?

What figures would be in your caring inner wisdom committee?

Can you let yourself fall into their strength and support and trust that you can do this?

HOW TO GRIEVE

Take your pain, your anger, your sadness
Place it in a cauldron of your tears
Warm it over the fire of self-compassion
And sit with it.

Watch it boil and bubble
Let it simmer and reduce
Stir it with kindness
Stay with it, patiently.

I cannot tell you how long it will take
But with its own sacred timing
One day you will realise
That it has evaporated –
Dissolved into the oneness.

And all that is left is
Love.

ON GRIEVING

There are many losses to grieve through life – and not just through bereavement. Grieving the loss of youth; grieving the childhood you'd wished you had; grieving for a relationship that has ended; grieving being misunderstood as a sensitive soul in an often-unkind world.

But how to grieve them?

In working with my own emotional wounds from childhood I kept looking for advice on *how* to grieve. I got frustrated. Why can't someone just give me a clear, step-by-step process that I can follow and be done with it?!

Of course, that is not how the human heart works. Grief and sorrow are complex and we each of us will have our own unique experience of them and they will move at their own rhythm in our lives.

But if I were to sum up what's needed in one word, it would be: *time*. Yes, I know. Frustrating, isn't it? And alongside time, you will need mindful awareness of how you're feeling, much warmth and kindness towards yourself, plenty of patience and perhaps also an ability to reflect on and find the wisdom in what you're experiencing.

As Queen Elizabeth II astutely said: 'grief is the price we pay for love'. So whether your grief is for a person, a pet, a way of being, or your hopes and dreams, how would it be to reframe it as evidence of your ability to love both others, yourself and life itself deeply?

Remind yourself that the presence of grief is evidence of your warm and loving heart: proof of your essential goodness and that love is your true nature.

STRONG FOUNDATIONS

May you learn to see yourself
May you learn to hear yourself
May you learn to love yourself
So that you no longer need to search and grasp in vain
Ever-hungry to fill the infinite hole
Left gaping from not being seen, heard or loved
By those who should have, without question,
But did not.

SELF-WORTH

Knowing that you are, fundamentally, a good person can offer a profound sense of refuge in difficult times.

Though for many of us, *believing* this can prove challenging.

No matter what we've done, how much we love others and what we've achieved, underneath it all there may still be a nagging sense of not feeling good enough.

The reasons for this may be numerous – though I suspect most of them will have their root in childhood.

Being scolded, shamed, ridiculed or ignored by parents or carers; being bullied or mocked by teachers or peers; having done things that you now regret; being told over and over that you're 'too sensitive'. All of these and more can leave a residue of shame.

You may feel inadequate, inferior or useless, like you don't quite measure up. You never feel good enough.

You lack self-worth.

Self-worth can be defined as a sense of one's own value as a human being'[7].

It's an internal sense of being good enough. It incorporates the sense that you are worthy of love from others.

Self-worth does not need markers of success; it does not require external validation.

---

[7] merriam-webster.com/dictionary/self-worth

It's a feeling that you are fundamentally a good person no matter how others treat you or the mistakes you make or the successes you experience.

Self-worth is an unshakeable belief in your essential goodness and that you have a right to be here.

But unfortunately, too many of us struggle to believe this. You too?

So how do we develop self-worth when that belief in our essential goodness is lacking?

It may be a long journey, but you can start by becoming a friend to yourself; by being on our own side.

This means being encouraging and kind to yourself – daily.

A daily practice to nurture self-worth

Look at yourself in the mirror … look deep into your eyes … and say out loud:

I am worthy of respect.

I am a good person with a lot to offer.

I am loving.

I am enough.

Make this a daily spiritual practice of devotion to yourself.

Keep saying this to yourself even if it feels icky or false or embarrassing.

Learn to talk to yourself with appreciation and kindness.

And one day, I promise, you will feel a shift.

And when you do, notice where and how you feel it in your body – and let that feeling sink into you as you sink into it.

Marinate in feeling a good and worthy person.

And may you move through life rooted in the strongest foundations of self-worth, compassion and love.

ASK YOURSELF THIS

Each morning
Before the hooks of other people's energy
Attach themselves onto your heart and mind,
Ask yourself this:
How do I feel?

Each time
You find yourself erased
By other people's demands,
Ask yourself this:
What do I need?

Each moment
You feel a flash of intuition
Rising from your inner depths,
Ask yourself this:
What is my soul yearning for?

And use your precious answers
To honour your feelings
To meet your needs
To trust the wise whispers of your soul
And day by day, step by step
To build a life
As sovereign of your own realm.

HOW DO YOU FEEL & WHAT DO YOU NEED?

It can be strangely challenging to find the words to describe how you're feeling. So here are some prompts to help.

How do you feel? Here are some words for **physical feelings & sensations**:

Achy	Heavy	Sleepy
Alert	Hollow	Slow
Bloated	Hot	Sore
Blocked	Jumpy	Spacey
Breathless	Knotted	Spacious
Brittle	Lethargic	Sparkly
Buzzy	Light	Stiff
Clammy	Loose	Still
Clenched	Nauseous	Suffocated
Cold	Numb	Tender
Constricted	Open	Tense
Contracted	Prickly	Throbbing
Dizzy	Pulsing	Tight
Drained	Queasy	Tingly
Dull	Radiant	Tired
Empty	Relaxed	Trembly
Expansive	Rigid	Twitchy
Floating	Sensitive	Vibrant
Fluttery	Settled	Warm
Gentle	Shaky	Wired
Grounded	Shivery	Wobbly

And here are some words for your **emotional & mental state:**

Abandoned	Fearless	Overwhelmed
Aggressive	Focused	Passionate
Angry	Foggy	Pessimistic
Anxious	Frightened	Powerful
Ashamed	Grateful	Present
Awkward	Grounded	Productive
Bored	Guilty	Rageful
Brave	Happy	Regal
Calm	Imaginative	Sad
Clear	Insecure	Secure
Composed	Intuitive	Sensitive
Confused	Jittery	Sexy
Content	Joyful	Sociable
Creative	Judgmental	Soulful
Critical	Lost	Spacey
Delighted	Loving	Spiritual
Depressed	Manic	Stressed
Disconnected	Mean	Strong
Distracted	Melancholic	Tired
Dreamy	Mellow	Visionary
Excited	Mischievous	Vulnerable
Exhausted	Numb	Wistful
Fearful	Optimistic	Worried

What do you need today?

What's non-negotiable for your physical, emotional, mental and spiritual wellbeing?

This is about the need for safety and security. For nutrition and hydration. For movement and rest. For friendship and support and healthy relationships as well as the need to be seen, heard and valued, and the need for creative expression and spiritual connection.

Again, here are just a few suggestions:

Alone time

Be with other people

Chat with a friend

Chocolate

Creating/crafting

Cup of tea or coffee

Dance

Go out

Hugs

Journalling

Lie down

Meditate

Nap

Nature

Nutritious food

Paint

Prayer

Read

Rest

Run

Scream

Sex

Stay in

Stretch

Support from your partner

Walk

Water

Writing

And what is your soul yearning for?

Perhaps journal on it.

Start with the words '*My soul is yearning for…*' and write whatever comes up.

SEARING

The white-hot pain
She thought
Was killing her
Was, in fact,
The soul forge flame
Branding her heart
So she could return
As the Warrior Queen
She truly is.

GO GENTLY

It hurts, I know. It hurts to finally turn to face the difficult feelings from which you have been hiding away for so long.

There may be oceans of tears. There may be earthquakes of anger. There may be caverns of sorrow.

You may be afraid that you'll get stuck or overwhelmed if you let the feelings in.

But, my love, the only way out is through. And the only way through is to feel what you need to feel and ask these feelings what they have to say and what they need from you.

I'm not saying it's easy. Go gently dear one. Treat yourself like a precious object.

But if you can find a way to let yourself feel what needs to be felt then you will discover a greater sense of inner peace within your heart and soul.

Whether that's talking to a friend or a therapist or writing it out in your journal; whether it's sitting in front of your altar or in a church and offering it over to whatever presence you sense as the divine (if any); whether it's pummelling a pillow or meditating in peace – or perhaps a combination of all of these – processing your feelings will help you to feel better.

It will help you understand yourself more deeply. It will bring healing.

And perhaps you may reach a place where you are able to consider the emotional pain and turmoil, the grief and sorrow, the anger and frustration as being the refining fire and the alchemical flames that will enable you to rise stronger than before.

COURAGE

You can be strong
Without needing
To barricade your heart
Behind impenetrable
Defences.

Your heart
Is the source
Of courage.

So take off your armour
And soften into
The loving strength
Of your heart
And let
Its power
Lead the way.

YOUR COURAGEOUS HEART

We humans expend so much energy on holding on, don't we? We hold on to fears, disappointments, resentments, grief, anger and frustration. We hold on to ideas of how things 'should' be. Clinging to what feels good; fearful in case it disappears. Pushing away what we don't want.

All this holding on may cause us to build up emotional armoury within our body, manifesting in muscle and joint tension, discomfort and pain, and a nervous system set to hypervigilant mode.

And, most painful of all, we build up impenetrable defences around our hearts, determined not to let ourselves get hurt again. We may become guarded, snippy, cynical, withdrawn. We lose trust in others. And we lose trust in the wisdom of living life with an open heart.

It doesn't feel good.

Yes, living with an open heart leaves us vulnerable to being hurt. But the alternative is a life half-lived: safe but numb, protected but unfulfilled.

Let us remember the origins of the word courage come from *'cor'* the Latin word for heart. And so it is in the portal of your heart that you will find the courage to love freely and deeply.

Yes, you may have been hurt before. Yes, you may feel you have failed before.

But it is your heart's energy that enables you, indeed it *encourages* you, to embrace life and its challenges and love it all anyway.

THE FORGE

This pain
This anguish
This grief
They are the fire
The anvil
The hammer
Through which
Your soul is being wrought
In the forge
Of life
And soon
You will be
Ready
Reformed
And reborn.

ON SMITHCRAFT

Let us consider the ancient art of smithcraft.

In a blacksmith's forge, the smith takes her raw material of iron and plunges it into burning coals and holds it there until it becomes red hot and pliable.

With care, she takes the glowing metal and hammers it into shape on the anvil.

But the job is not complete with one visit to the fire!

Oh no, she must work slowly and mindfully.

Moving back and forth between the fire and her anvil.

Gradually, with care, she crafts the iron with the blows of her hammer.

Working steadily, trusting in the process … until, with its own perfect timing, the piece has been worked to completion.

And this is what you are experiencing when you are in the underworld of difficult times, being worked by your sorrow and grief.

You are being called to allow yourself to be worked by the process; to allow yourself to become pliable in the fires of this soul forge; to shed the layers which are no longer in alignment with your truth; to keep going no matter how hard it feels; to trust in the process; to remould yourself and rebirth yourself in your new and unique form.

Your soul's truth.

LOST AND FOUND

Deep in the cave
Of not knowing
A glimmer
Caught her eye
And there,
Amidst the rubble
Of her life,
She unearthed
A buried jewel.
Multi-faceted and exquisite,
Radiant and unique:
She'd found
Her soul.

FINDING YOURSELF

In many religions and wisdom traditions the spiritual journey is upwards: a drive to rise above the world and transcend this earthly life and our bodies; to merge with the Oneness of spirit, perhaps to meet God in the heavens above.

But what of *inscendence*[8]? That is, the drive to move inwards, into the core of this earthly life and our inner depths.

This is the journey to your soul.

This is the journey to the sacred essence of *you*: your deepest self and the unique characteristics and qualities that define you.

You won't find your soul looking outside yourself. Nor will you connect with your soul pursuing spiritual practices that seek to transcend your body.

Perhaps you can only meet this essential aspect of yourself when you dive deep below your surface self into the underworld of the mystery of your psyche.

Perhaps you must first lose sight of your surface self to finally find and appreciate your true self.

What if this was the true gift of plumbing the depths and feeling so intensely?

That is: the gift of rediscovering that precious and radiant jewel that is your soul.

---

[8] A term used by Thomas Berry, a priest, cultural historian and scholar, and expanded upon by the depth psychologist, wilderness guide and author Bill Plotkin.

THE FLAME

And in the bleakest moment,
Overcome by the pain
Of sorrow, loneliness and grief,
I closed my eyes.
Wishing it would just stop.
Longing for oblivion.
Praying for release through my tears.
Giving up.

And that is when I saw it.
A candle flame,
In my mind's eye,
Glowing
In the grey-cold stone tomb of my sadness.
A steady dancing light gleamed
That I immediately knew
Would never be extinguished.

And I felt it
As an answer to my prayer.
My soul whispering to me
Of the perpetual flame
Always with me and within me
Waiting for me to tend it:
The flame of hope
And life.

SURRENDERING

I wonder whether it's when we surrender to our emotional pain that we create the space for healing to occur. I wonder whether it's when we let go of the struggle and stop pretending that all is okay that we can finally be honest with ourselves. I wonder whether it's when we stop resisting our difficult feelings that they can finally flow through us, be felt and understood.

When we surrender, we are finally honouring those parts of ourselves that we've hitherto rejected, silenced and shamed for too long. Our anger. Our jealousy. Our ambition. Our embarrassment. Our regret. Our guilt. Our shame.

Every one of us just wants to be listened to; to be seen and heard. We long for affirmation that what we're experiencing is real and true and that it's okay to feel what we're feeling. But perhaps this is something we must offer to ourselves – because if we're relying on receiving that affirmation solely from external sources then we may be waiting a long time. And in the meantime, our suffering continues.

So perhaps it's time to surrender. To give up the fight and invite the pain in.

I know it may feel bleak and desolate and frightening. But perhaps it's when we let go of our coping mechanisms, our pretending, and our ego defences that the soul can finally speak to us – because we are ready to hear.

Your soul will never give up on you. Your soul is ready and waiting to comfort you.

If only you can drop the defences and hear its whispers. Can you hear it calling you?

REASONS TO KEEP GOING

The rose-gold thrill of a full moon rising in a denim sky.
The glitter of dragon flies dancing in the late-summer sun.
The candy floss exuberance of cherry blossom.
The sleek softness of a cat as it glides past beneath my hand.
The twilight song of a robin atop my favourite tree.
The abundant blooms and heady scent of roses.
The blaze of a winter sunset warming me from within.
The fractals of bare oak branches against an ice-blue sky.
The helpless giggles when only my beloved and I know what we're laughing about.

These are just a few things
I'm thinking of today
As reasons to keep going.

LOOK AROUND YOU

When you're stuck in your head or spiralling through intensely difficult feelings, you may lose your connection to the sensual world.

When you're looking down at the well-worn tracks of self-critical thoughts, of anxious fretting, of depressive hopelessness ... you may forget to look up and see the good around you.

And most times when you look up, you can find something beautiful in your environment; something that delights your senses; something that takes you out of your head and into connection with the people and world around you.

Recognise beauty and feel how you respond to it.

Lean into your ability to notice the finer details and subtle energies around you and take a few moments consciously to feel them deeply.

Use all the senses that are available to you.

See the beauty of a flower.

Hear the sound of music or birdsong.

Feel the comforting touch of clothes against your skin or touch a tree or leaf or a soft blanket.

Smell the scent of flowers or your coffee.

Taste your food as you eat it or consciously eat some chocolate or whatever treats you enjoy and really savour the flavour.

Notice how you respond when you do this; notice how your spirit is uplifted and your soul expands.

There are many places to find beauty in your life – large and small.

Even the everyday things that you usually take for granted, such as the colour of the grass outside; raindrops sliding down a pane of glass; the comfort of your favourite chair; even the beautiful functionality of the curves on a tap or door handle – yes really!

Slowing down to truly notice beauty and taking it in through your senses will light up parts of your brain related to satisfaction and fulfilment and prompt the release of feel-good chemicals such as dopamine and opioids (which also muffle your perception of pain)[9].

So slow down and reflect on what simple pleasures bring you joy.

Look around you now and take in the simple beauties in your immediate environment; the shapes and textures and forms as well as the sights and sounds and scents.

Notice how they make you feel – and invite these feelings to sink into you as you savour them.

Consider what enchants you and helps you feel contented: and may these delights become your reasons to keep going.

Write them down overleaf and let them be your medicine bag to dip into when it all feels too much.

---

[9] *Hardwiring Happiness* by Rick Hanson.

This page is intentionally left blank so you can write down – and add to – your list of reasons to keep going; the simple pleasures that bring you joy:

HEART FIRE

When the demons
Of feeling not good enough
Of thinking you're a bad person
Of feeling guilty, worthless and ashamed
Haunt your dark places,

Can you turn towards
The hearthfire within
Your heart?

Can you let yourself be healed
By this inner flame
That illuminates the darkness?
That offers you love, compassion and peace?

Rest here awhile
And feel this
Infinite, unconditional love
Burning brightly and warmly,
Welcoming you
Home.

SOURCING LOVE

When you're in the midst of difficult times, feeling low or overwhelmed it's good to lean into the support of those who love you: family and friends, maybe even a pet. But it's also helpful to be able to source support from the one person who will unfailingly be with you all your life: yourself.

It's useful to have a practice to fall back on that helps you to feel peaceful, contented and loving, even on the darkest of days.

Here is one such practice; it guides you to source a sense of loving connection within and all around you:

Light a candle (or use an LED candle, image or video of a candle) and gaze into its flame… Let this candle flame be a source of love… And imagine its warmth filling your heart.

Imagine it igniting a sacred flame within you of self-compassion and self-worth and self-understanding.

Sit with peace. Open to a sense that you are all right, right now. You are safe. You are protected by the walls around you.

Sit with contentment. Invite a gentle sense of gratitude for all that you have and all that you are, and the enoughness of this moment.

Sit with love. Know that you are connected to the web of life, to all living things. How would it be to feel held by this web?

And invite the flame before you and the flame within you to be infused with peace, contentment and love, and become a source of comfort and solace that you can carry deep within you, always.

THE COMPANY I KEEP

Sinking into loneliness,
Heavy grief
Weighing down
My heart,
I notice
Through the window
The flowers watching me.
And I am lifted
By the remembrance
Of the living spirit
Of the world around me.
And as I gaze
At the flowers and leaves
The clouds and trees
I feel welcomed
Back into the arms
Of the loving family
Who were there with me
All along.

SACRED NATURE

Do you feel part of the natural world ... or is nature something that is 'out there'?

The dictionary definition of nature is: 'the phenomena of the physical world collectively, including plants, animals, the landscape, and other features and products of the earth, as opposed to humans or human creations'.

It explicitly puts humans outside the realm of nature.

Yet are we not also a product of the earth?

Are we not created from the same elements?

Are we not sustained by the food that is grown in the earth?

Are we not also a physical phenomenon that inhabits this planet?

This is not how humanity has always regarded nature.

Surely our ancestors would not have had the deluded arrogance to set humanity apart from nature. For it behoved them to live in necessary respect for their environment and the seasons, because their lives depended on it.

They had to find their own food, and in later times, grow and nurture and harvest it.

They needed to understand the signs and signals of changing weather patterns.

If they did not show respect for their place in the living web of life, then they would suffer or even die.

Perhaps it was not until Yahweh of the Hebrew scriptures was presented as the creator and ruler of the cosmos that humans conceived of the idea that they were not part of nature.

Perhaps it was only since it was decreed that this distant Father-figure appointed man to be the ruler of nature – 'you have given him dominion over the works of your hands; you have put all things under his feet'[10] – that mankind set himself above the natural world and sought to tame and control it and consider it a God-given resource to utilise and, since the industrial revolution, to plunder.

And so perhaps it is of no surprise that we humans often feel lost and alone, yearning to belong.

But how wonderful it is to remember that we *do* belong!

We belong to the family of living beings that inhabits this beautiful animate Earth. We are part of nature. Our cells are made of billion-years-old elements, and we are fed and sustained by the Earth and the Sun.

How would it be to look out of your window now and see the sky, the clouds, the birds, the trees as your kinfolk?

How would it be to walk on the earth and greet the plants and flowers, even the rocks and stones, as your sisters and brothers?

How would it be to lie down on the ground and feel held by your mother – by Mother Earth herself?

Try it.

Look around you now.

---

[10] Psalm 8, 6:10

What can you see in your environment that reminds you that you are part of the family of all living beings?

Find something to connect with.

Perhaps a leaf, flower, cloud, rain or sunlight.

Gently gaze at it… Be with it… Open your heart to it.

And let it welcome you home.

EARTHED

Sit with Mother Earth
And you will come to know
That she is always with you.
Let her hold you.
Let her whisper to your heart.
Feel her rise through the soles of your feet
And take root in the soil of your soul.
She will guide you to strip away
The suffocating layers
And the painted masks
That have hidden your true self
For too long.

THE GREAT MOTHER

The archetype of the Great Mother is powerful and deeply rooted in the human psyche. Cave paintings and sculpted female figures have been found in their thousands across numerous sites throughout Europe and North Asia, for example, some dating as far back as 30-40,000 years ago.

There is great comfort and solace to be found in connecting to the presence of a Great Mother, however she appears to you and whatever name you give her. Whether you find her walking in a wood, by the sea, or in your garden; whether you have an entire altar dedicated to her or just a statue representing her; whether you connect simply by lighting a candle; or however you feel called to, let her into your heart and she will comfort, protect and nurture you.

For the Great Mother loves you unconditionally and nothing you can say or do will make her love you any less. She is always there within and around you, a constant presence of love, nurturing, protection, empowerment and wisdom.

Perhaps She is most easily felt as Mother Earth in the soil, rocks and roots beneath your feet.

As you're sitting here, reading this book, can you sense the solid ground beneath you now?

Let your awareness travel down through the floor, through the foundations of the building you're in… Send your awareness down into the roots and rocks and soil… Exhale and sense your physical body relaxing, releasing, softening… Can you feel her support?

How would it be to let yourself be held by her; by Mother Earth?

YOU ARE HEALING

Be patient, dear one,
You are healing.
Keep walking
The labyrinth.
Each journey inwards
Takes you closer
To the root
Of your pain.
Each return
Brings you deeper
Into the healing wellspring
Of your heart.

Be patient, dear one,
These cycles
Are sacred.
Keep following them,
Keep journeying,
Keep going.
Because one day
You will look
Into your eyes
And see
Only love.

WHAT IS HEALING?

What does it mean to heal?

The word 'heal' is derived from an old English word of Germanic origin that means 'to restore to sound health'.

So, to heal invokes a sense of making something sound or healthy once again; a suggestion of a return to wholeness that in turn implies this wholeness is our natural state.

And while yes, this may be true to some extent, the trouble is that in the results-driven, competitive, too-often superficial culture in which we find ourselves, this urge to wholeness can become another means to judge ourselves, and, inevitably, to find ourselves wanting.

For what is healed and whole anyway?

And, perhaps most saliently, *who* gets to define this concept?

We must be careful that we are not holding up an ableist, privileged picture of what it means to be whole, and judging ourselves and others against that.

This picture of wellbeing too often looks white, thin, conventionally attractive, youthful, able-bodied and is based on a lifestyle that requires plentiful financial means to fund and sustain.

Further, it is worth reflecting on these words: *'It is no measure of health to be well adjusted to a profoundly sick society'*[11].

---

[11] Often attributed to the philosopher and teacher Krishnamurti, see kfoundation.org/it-is-no-measure-of-health-to-be-well-adjusted-to-a-profoundly-sick-society

Striving towards an idealised picture of physical and mental wellbeing is perilously entangled with a consumerist culture that manipulates us by selling the lie that if we buy this product or that service then all our ills will fade away.

Chasing the illusion of healed perfection also erases a truth about the nature of all of life.

We are not meant to be in the full bloom of summer all year round. Periods of lying fallow are natural and needed.

Remembering this can help us to let go of struggling to attain the impossible dream that one day all our problems will be fixed and that we'll live an eternally happy life, floating along on an even keel.

For life is not like that.

Perhaps it would be healthier to consider healing as a process of finding some kind of peace with what we have experienced and what we're experiencing now.

Perhaps the true healing journey is one from ignorance to understanding; from acting out from our unacknowledged emotional lacks and wounds to a place where we respond to challenges from a wiser perspective.

Perhaps it is when we have developed an inner ground of 'enoughness' and of feeling safe, contented and loved that we can consider that we truly understand what healing means.

For then we have a place to which we can return when we are inevitably knocked off balance by ill-health and physical pain, by disappointments and betrayals, by our own unhelpful thoughts and self-criticism.

Maybe healing is developing enough patient self-compassion so that you can finally look yourself in the mirror with eyes of love and know that this love will never leave you, no matter what happens in life.

THE BUD

What she thought
Was pain
Was the unexpected
Bud of hope
Opening
Inside her
Weary heart.

ON HOPE

Sometimes hope can feel painful. When we're accustomed to disappointment, to sorrow, to betrayal, to grief ... hope can feel like an affront to the pain we're experiencing.

How dare hope tease me with its desire for a different way of being? How dare hope mock me with the suggestion that I can follow my dreams? How dare hope goad me into believing that things can get better?

Yet to be human is to hope. And to hope is so very human.

Hope is a visceral experience: a flutter of excitement in the belly; a glittery feeling behind the eyes; an inner smile that expands through the body. Or an ache of longing in a weary heart.

Hope arises from our faculty of imagination. We humans create imaginary worlds. We tell stories. We anticipate what might come next. We imagine our lives into being. We foster dreams for the life we long for and these longings and dreams inspire the action required to bring into physical manifestation that which our hearts yearn for.

And all of this imagining is based on hope – the desire and expectation for something to happen.

If hope feels unexpected or painful for you, I invite you to reflect on these questions:

- Why does it feel painful to hope?
- What bud of hope is ready to open within you?
- What does this hope need to feel safe?
- What steps can you take to nurture this bud of hope so that it may gently open, at its own pace?

A PRAYER

May the Sun
Warm my heart
That was frozen
By unkindness.

May the Earth
Receive the tears
That feel like
They should not be shed.

May the Moon
Hear the whispers
That yearn
To be expressed.

And may I
Feel held
In a way
That I have never done before.

ON PRAYER

Many of us have a complicated relationship with prayer.

Perhaps because it is associated with a religion we were brought up in to which we no longer adhere. Maybe we do not trust there is anyone or anything listening. Or perhaps we have imbibed the cultural messaging to pull ourselves up by our bootstraps and only rely on ourselves.

All three of those were true for me.

Yet a prayer can be as simple as expressing an earnest desire or wish.

It does not have to be imparted to a deity or an external entity if this is not in line with your beliefs.

Express your prayer to yourself first of all, and perhaps this simple act of articulating your deepest wish will inspire you to work towards it.

Or maybe you might whisper your heart's longing to the Moon or offer it to a river or confide in a flower.

Because perhaps you don't have to only rely on yourself.

What if your kinfolk in nature *are* listening?

What if the invisible threads that connect us all are alive to your prayers and the act of speaking them resonates through the tapestry of life and changes the picture in ways you might never have imagined?

Or what if you *do* have a guardian angel or a soul guide who has been alongside you since before you were born, waiting for you to speak your soul's yearnings so they can help you?

What if...?

What if your prayers *were* answered?

Is it not worth the risk of speaking them?

At the very least, you will be honouring your heart's deepest longings even if you *are* the only person to hear and receive your prayers.

But who knows, perhaps unseen energies and beings *are* out there waiting to help you.

It all starts with a prayer…

Say a prayer now…

Sit somewhere peaceful, perhaps light a candle first.

And repeat the piece called '*A Prayer*' over and over – silently or out loud.

Call in the holding that you need.

Call to your own heart and soul.

Call to the Sun and Moon; call out to the elements; call to the divine; call out to the Great Mother – or to whatever figure or presence you wish to…

…And may your prayers be answered and may you feel held by love.

RETURNING

I have lain in winter's cave a while now.

I have wept, slept, dreamed and rested.

And now, as I open my eyes, I can feel the atmosphere has changed.

Even though it is still dark here my intuition tells me that the season has shifted. I can sense the awakening and promise of the earliest signs of spring.

And I feel different too. The heaviness has lifted. The weariness has faded. I feel more present and alert.

I can sense the loving presence of the Great Mother within my heart, and I feel stronger and clearer and ready to return.

There is a shaft of misty daylight shimmering into this place that I had not noticed before. And I realise it is showing me the way out; illuminating a pathway that I can see rises out of this place.

Now I know that I am ready to return to the surface; to re-engage with life with a renewed clarity and vision.

I have grieved.

I have faced the dreaded feelings and long-buried experiences and they have not killed me.

The hard knot of pain in my heart has transformed into a warm, tender yet fierce loving kindness and compassion for myself and all beings.

I am ready to return…

*

And now you are returning.

The poems and reflections in this final section offer you the strength and motivation to return and re-engage with life.

The pieces here invite you to shake off the shackles of old limiting beliefs and societal conditioning that keeps you small. They ask you to dig deep and embrace your wise and wild true self. They guide you to renewed clarity and vision. They encourage you to tend to the fire in your soul and to wholeheartedly embrace life.

So, are you ready now?

Are you ready to re-engage with life?

Are you ready to summon courage and wisdom, to be on your own side, and to try your best to live with an open heart?

For your capacity to feel deeply, to see into the intricacies of the human heart and soul and to empathise with the pain of others are gifts that this world needs. And they are gifts, when claimed, that will help you to live with greater meaning, purpose and satisfaction.

Let me guide you to summon the strength and presence that you need to stand tall with dignity, rooted in self-worth, as the wise, complex, compassionate and brilliantly sensitive being that you truly are!

THIS MUCH I KNOW

I know now
That until I speak
With my true voice
I will remain
Trapped
In an exhausting cycle
Of not knowing
Who I am
Or what I am
Here for;
Comparing myself to others
Finding myself wanting
And collapsing
Into discombobulating despair.

I know now
It is time
To stop
Hiding
My truth.

I have arrived
Here
At this point
In my life
And now I am ready
To acknowledge all
I have experienced
And I am ready

To speak.

I know now
That by sharing
My pain
I will feel
Less alone
And be a light
To others
In their darkness.

SPEAKING YOUR TRUTH

By sharing our stories, we feel less alone.

By speaking our truth, we can activate the truth in others.

By shining a light on our own dark places, we offer a lantern to help others illuminate what has been long been hidden within their depths.

However, in a culture where you're encouraged to keep calm and carry on and a society where happiness is the ultimate goal, speaking of your grief and sorrow, your frustrations and disappointments, your wounds and pain can be difficult.

You may be worried that you'll be judged (you probably will be).

You may be anxious that you'll be told you've got nothing to complain about (you probably will be).

You may be nervous that you'll be wilfully misunderstood (you probably will be).

You may be apprehensive of being accused of being ungrateful or too sensitive or that you're over-sharing (you probably will be).

Because unfortunately many of us are just not very adept at talking about feelings. I'm from England – birthplace of stiff upper-lipped stoicism where we still largely don't talk about how we truly feel.

It takes emotional maturity both to be able to talk about how we feel and to hear how our behaviour has impacted others.

Too often other family members don't have this level of emotional maturity and will accuse you of criticising or blaming them if you share how their words and conduct have landed with you.

Your honesty – even when carefully expressed with compassion and without blame – may activate unconscious wounds in others and they'll go on the attack because they lack the self-awareness to realise something has triggered them and their reaction is out of all proportion to the current situation.

Nevertheless, I believe that by sharing the truth of our feelings and experience with tender and fierce compassion towards ourselves and others we can contribute both to our own and to collective healing. That's because by sharing our stories we help ourselves and others to feel seen and heard – a fundamental human emotional need.

Start simply and with an audience who is likely to be sympathetic.

You might not yet feel ready to talk to your mother about how her constant criticism has hurt you, for example, but you could express your feelings through writing in a journal – for your eyes only.

Or you might talk with an empathetic family member, friend or colleague, or a therapist if you have the financial resources for that.

In time you might feel called to share your unique story through messages on social media, a newsletter, poetry or even in a book.

What life experiences might you share to be a light to help someone else in troubled times?

SOME PEOPLE

Some people mistake sensitivity for weakness
Some people assume calm equals placid
Some people dismiss quietness as emptiness.

Meanwhile, I watch and listen, I feel and notice
Meanwhile, I reflect in order to better understand
Meanwhile, I wait until I am ready to speak.

Some people don't understand the power
That sensitivity, calm and quiet
Brings to a soul that burns brightly
For love of truth, justice and life,

And the undervalued potency
In biding your time
Until what needs to be said
Pours forth with radiant power.

YOU ARE NEEDED

Life can feel challenging for people who feel deeply, notice the subtleties in life and who are empathetic.

We live in a world of open-plan workspaces, of group work, of noise, stimulation, aggression and pushiness. And the world bombards us with constant stimulation through proliferating forms of media, including the ubiquitous smartphone.

Perhaps you can find solace in the thought that your tendency to experience life intensely and challenging emotions deeply, comes with the ability to feel joy and love and fun and radiant happiness much more deeply too.

But if that feels like a distant possibility, remember that life is not a linear journey from A to B. Life is a spiral of twists and turns and ups and downs and ins and outs ... and none of it lasts forever. All things change. Especially your emotions.

As a sensitive person you have gifts of insight, intuition, reflection, measured responses, and appreciation of the inter-connectedness of life. You are one of the wise counsellors, creatives and peace-bringers that this world sorely needs.

And if your sensitivity – or any aspect of you – has been misunderstood or used against you, may you offer yourself the tender and fierce balm of self-compassion.

May you accept your sensitivity.

May you find the strength in it.

And may you unlock its undoubted power.

LESSONS

When doubt comes
May it teach you the power of questioning.

When anger comes
May it teach you the power of clear boundaries.

When fear comes
May it teach you the power of freedom.

When grief comes
May it teach you the power of your heart.

And may your doubt lead to clarity.
May your anger lead to action.
May your fear lead to courage.
May your grief lead to love.

And may you accept all of this and more
Into the guest house of your body-mind
So that you may live wholeheartedly
Welcoming all that you are.

ACCEPTANCE

Acceptance is a useful skill to cultivate in life.

I'm not talking about giving up to grim defeat or approving of things that go against your values, and I'm not suggesting you collapse into apathy.

No, what I'm speaking of is accepting the reality of what is in the moment and the feelings you have about that. And that includes accepting what you cannot change and the frustration and grief that may accompany that.

Maybe you have lost a loved one. Maybe a friend has betrayed you. Maybe you're upset by an unfair situation at work. Maybe you're full of anger and grief at the destruction of local woodland and how it is symptomatic of the wider devastation of the delicate ecosystems on this Earth.

Whatever the cause, I invite you to accept your feelings and to let them flow through you, so you don't get stuck and contracted into hopeless despair.

Instead try to remain open to spaciousness and freedom by accepting your feelings so you can keep moving forward through life.

Ultimately this is about accepting yourself – all parts and layers of you.

The anger and sadness, the flippancy and defensiveness, as well as the deeper layers that feel vulnerable, needy and scared.

I've experienced how accepting that which feels challenging or scary or shameful creates a feeling of release and freedom as the contraction of resistance subsides.

And this acceptance makes space for the parts of you that are loving and kind, joyful and playful, creative and purposeful, wise and caring, to spontaneously flow into your heart and mind.

But when we continue to reject our feelings, we close down and contract around a scared core whose vulnerability we defend at all costs.

And this contraction and closing down comes at the cost of losing touch with our passions and enthusiasms and our deepest heartfelt longings.

We cannot make space for joy without also allowing space for grief.

Otherwise we wind up allowing only a very narrow range of feeling – a safe but dreary life of dulled emotion and anxious avoidance.

There is a famous poem by the 13th-century Persian poet, Rumi, that describes being human as 'a guest house'[12] and how every day there is a new arrival of joys and sorrows, and he advises us to 'welcome and entertain them all':

> *The dark thought, the shame, the malice,*
> *meet them at the door laughing,*
> *and invite them in.*
>
> *Be grateful for whoever comes,*
> *because each has been sent*
> *as a guide from beyond.*

---

[12] *The Guest House* By Jalāl al-Dīn Rūmī as translated by Coleman Barks.

…Because they 'may be clearing you out for some new delight'.

So, when we welcome all emotional visitors to the guest house of our body-mind we are ensuring the door is always open to joy, passion and a life lived wholeheartedly.

NAMING THE PARTS

Confused little girl.
Mischievous pixie.
Fiery spirit.
Derided daughter.
Numb victim.
Magical child.
Rebellious teenager.
Hungry ghost.
Fierce Priestess.
Unlimited Creatrix.
Angry witch.
Courageous seeker and speaker of truth.

Curious Maiden.
Nurturing Mother.
Sovereign Queen.
Wise Crone.
Love beyond measure.

These are just some of the parts I have met within me.
The parts that I now welcome to dwell within the vastness of who I am.
I wonder whether seeing, acknowledging, listening to and accepting all parts of ourselves is what enables us to heal; is what makes us whole?

THE INNER FAMILY

We humans are all a collection of different parts. We are each of us both one person *and* multitudes.

We are the sum of our life experience so far. And all those parts of ourselves at every age still live within us. Some may be quite young, others teenage, others adult. Some of them may feel happy and content, empowered and strong. Others may feel vulnerable and need your kind attention.

We naturally understand this because it's common to say things like 'a part of me wants to go out today but another part of me wants to stay home and relax on the sofa'.

As I write this book, there's a part of me fretting that nobody will read it and another part who is gritty and knows she has something to share of value and will ensure she does all she can to get this book into the hands of people who need it.

You could view these parts as your *inner family* – a group of beings who each has their own views and standpoints and experiences, but they are all related. And you – your adult self here in this moment – is head of the family.

Acknowledging the parts of you that feel strong and capable is empowering and can be a source of inner strength and resilience when you feel down and defeated. And communicating with the more vulnerable parts with love, compassion and encouragement can bring healing and integration to your whole self.

Who dwells within *you*? What do they need? Listen to them. And perhaps one day, you will even learn to love them.

LET GO (III)

She was glad
That she'd learned
To let go.

For what she'd feared
Was a limitless dangerous darkness
Was, in fact, the quiet nurturing cave
Of her soul.

And now she knows
That in each letting go
She falls deeper
Into the infinite source
Of loving trust
Within her heart.

Returning

THE GIFT OF LETTING GO

Have you spent some time in your soul sanctuary with your inner wisdom committee? (See pages 103-5.)

If so, how has it felt to let go of contracting around a scared core and surrender to trusting in a more spacious, strong and wise place within you?

I wonder whether, having let go of resisting your feelings, needs and desires, you've been able to land in this refuge and experience at least a taste of the healing power of letting yourself be there?

I wonder whether having connected to your inner resources that you've found the strength to feel what you'd feared to let yourself feel?

I know that when I let go of the struggle and connect to my anger and grief that I land in a place that ultimately feels healing and soulful – though I'll often resist and find myself reaching for the distraction-machine that is my smartphone. A sure sign that I'm getting close to touching a painful place that needs my compassionate attention.

And now I have been to these once-feared places, I have finally realised that they won't destroy me.

Instead, I have realised that they are home to parts of me that need my attention.

For example, I'll often find a sad and lonely child-version of me there who needs love and comfort and to know that she's not alone.

And then I'll give her/myself a hug, stroke her/my cheek and whisper comforting words, such as:

'There there… I know, it's hard. It hurts, doesn't it? It's okay, I'm here now. I see you. I believe you.

I feel your pain. It's okay to feel what you're feeling.

You're not alone. Can you sense me with you?

It's okay to feel sad or angry, lost or rejected.

It's okay. I don't love you any less when you feel this way.

What do you need?

I'm here for you now. I love you.

Nothing you could do or say will ever stop me from loving you.

It's okay. I'm here, I am with you…'

Tears will often come – those most healing of Mother Nature's waters.

But I'll feel better for crying.

And each time I do this, I know I am building a solid foundation of safety deep within my being.

I am learning to regulate my nervous system.

I am developing trust between me and my inner child parts.

I am mothering myself.

I am drawing on and refilling the infinite source of love that flows from my heart and soul.

This is the true gift of learning to let go: rediscovering the wellspring of healing love that comes from within and is sourced from our connection to the ocean of love that is the mystery of life.

May you receive this gift of healing love.

May you feel this gift ever flowing to you and within you.

And may you live trusting in the loving presence of your heart and soul.

RETURNING

So she lay herself down
On Mother Earth's green mantle,
And her heart beat in rhythm
With the pulse of the planet,
Her blood flowed
With the tides of the moon,
Her bones became as strong
As the rocks, roots and trees,
Her soul soared
With the birds in the sky.

And as the Great Mother held her
She knew now
That she would never again be defeated
Because she had become the mother to herself
She never truly had.

Returning

MOTHERING YOURSELF

It is a sad fact to acknowledge, but nevertheless true: not all of us received the parenting we needed as children.

For many and complex reasons, some parents/carers cannot provide the full depth, consistency and quality of support to their offspring that every child needs to survive and flourish. And that vulnerable, wounded inner child stays within our psyche into adulthood.

Can you feel her? A younger version of you who is trapped in the confusing world of childhood. That part of you who feels little, lost, lonely and confused.

You may not be consciously aware of her but, like me, perhaps you've suffered from some of these issues. Low self-esteem. Anxiety. Depression. Chronic people-pleasing. Seeking external validation. Poor boundaries. Numbness. A loss of your own voice.

It's as if you have a hole in your soul: a vast sense of inner emptiness that you don't know how to begin to fill.

This is the language of that wounded little version of you. Because she's still there. Watching. Waiting. Needing to be loved.

But we can learn to re-parent our inner child.

We can learn to comfort ourselves by self-soothing.

We can learn to be there for ourselves by checking in with how we're feeling.

We can learn ways to regulate our anxious nervous system[13].

We can learn to nurture ourselves and be attentive to our needs and desires.

We can learn to protect ourselves through developing and communicating healthy boundaries.

We can be our own cheerleader by recognising our achievements and good qualities.

And we can become our own nurturing home base by always being there for ourselves. By tuning in to our inner child self and asking her what she needs. By ensuring we listen to her, love her and help her to feel safe, seen and supported so she can relax.

But it is also comforting to remember that there is another mother always present, always holding us, always with us.

And that is Mother Earth.

The strong, nurturing, stable presence beneath your feet.

I find sensing into this loving strength beneath me and around me is enormously comforting.

And with this comfort comes a reminder that my vulnerable inner child is only one part of me.

Like Mother Earth, I too can be strong and capable, loving and kind, wise and nurturing.

When I invoke this mother energy within myself, my scared inner child relaxes and in doing so she morphs back into her

---

[13] For example, *Anchored* by Deb Dana contains a treasure trove of information and ways to befriend your nervous system.

true nature: the magical, creative, divine child that lives in all our hearts.

Next time you get the chance, sit or lie down on the earth.

And let yourself be held by Her, Mother Earth – the Great Mother of us all.

Feel Her loving presence and strength within your heart and bones.

And know that you are not alone.

Tune into the Mother Earth's protective presence with this visualisation[14] – you may like to record yourself reading it:

Either sit somewhere indoors where you can be undisturbed or sit outdoors, perhaps near a tree.

As you sit, imagine or become aware of the ground covered with green grass all around you – surrounding you…

Feel into its nurturing, protective energy…

And imagine now that you can draw this green mantle around you – like a cloak of protection…

Feel its heaviness and warmth over your shoulders and cloaking your body…

Draw its hood over your head…

Feel protected by this green mantle and affirm to yourself: *'I am protected, always'*.

And know that whenever you need to, you can psychically draw this green mantle of protection around you.

---

[14] Thank you to Priestess Marion Brigantia for this meditation.

AND THEN

All her life
She'd looked outside herself
For approval
For validation
To confirm that she existed.

And then
She discovered the Inner Mother
The source of unconditional love
Within her soul.

She met her inside
Her pain, her grief, her anger.
She found her
In her own heart.

And now
The only approval she seeks
Is to look in the mirror
And see her own loving eyes looking back.

And so
Every morning she decides:
'I like who I am
I approve of me.
And that is enough'.

START THE DAY THIS WAY

How many times a day do you look in the mirror? What do you say to the image reflecting back?

Maybe they're just casual neutral glances or perhaps you criticise your clothes, your body, your hair, your face... Or maybe you avoid mirrors if you can because you don't like some aspect of the way you look.

How would it be to stand in front of a mirror and simply look into your own eyes? How would it be to look beyond the condition of your skin and hair ... and beyond the self-judgment? How would it be to look into your eyes and truly see yourself, as if for the first time?

I've found there is something deeply grounding, centring and healing in looking into my own eyes. I come back to myself. I can sense all parts of myself. I feel more self-accepting, self-aware and self-compassionate. I feel like I've come home.

It has long been said that the eyes are the windows to the soul. So, look deep into your eyes and see your spirit, your life energy, your uniqueness, your wisdom, your joy, your radiance: your soul.

Start the day this way:

Every morning, look yourself in the mirror and say to yourself, out loud:

'I like who I am. I approve of me. And that is enough'.

You might squirm a little at first. You might hear an unkind inner voice of mockery and doubt. But keep saying it each day. Then one day you will find you truly mean it.

RIP UP THE SCRIPT

Her life had seemed a script
Written by someone
Who had no knowledge of her.

This script lacked direction
And the more she tried to follow it
The more out of place she felt.

So she walked off the stage
Ripped up the script
And began to write her own directions.

Her soul knew the way
She'd just needed to realise
It was ready to guide her
All along.

Returning

WHOSE LIFE IS IT ANYWAY?

It's not uncommon to get to a point in our life where we stop and look back and wonder, *how did I get here?*

Why am I *here*?

Is *this* what I *truly* wanted?

For it is all too easy to fall into following the script that familial and societal expectations provide you.

A script that will largely be determined by your gender, cultural heritage, social class, financial means – and perhaps the unlived life of your parents or carers.

But what if your soul had a different agenda?

What if you were born with a calling?

What if you were born to share something with the world that only *you* can?

In this world view, your soul knows what you're here for. It knows the potential you carry within you and will guide and nudge you to follow pathways that will help you to remember.

This idea of calling is an ancient and longstanding one that can be traced from Plato in Ancient Greece to modern depth psychologists such as James Hillman.

From Plato's *Myth of Er* to Hillman's acorn theory (articulated in his book *The Soul's Code*) this notion of calling proposes that, before birth, your soul selects a purpose for you to fulfil during this time on Earth. It then passes through the Plain of Oblivion and drinks from Lethe, the river of forgetfulness.

And then you are born, forgetful of your purpose.

But you are also born with a 'daimon': a spiritual guide; a guiding image; a vision that you carry within. Your innate potential. And this daimon or guiding image will prompt you to find and follow the path that aligns your life with your calling.

Tending to the soul then is choosing to listen to your deep longings and yearnings and to develop the courage to follow them, even when they don't make sense, or they challenge the ego's desire to fit in and follow the path of least resistance.

Your calling isn't necessarily expressed through work by the way, though it may be. Perhaps it could simply be your way of being in the world rather than what you do[15]. Such as being compassionate, truthful, creative, inquisitive, ever-curious, or deeply loving.

Those of us with a more sensitive nature seem to have an innate understanding that there is a deeper meaning to life beyond superficial materialism.

We yearn to discover our purpose and will spend much time and energy seeking it because we long to live a more fulfilling and authentic life in alignment with our deepest values and dreams.

How is *your* soul calling to you to pay attention?

Have you felt the call to rip up the script and start again?

What aspects of your life would you like to rewrite?

---

[15] A perspective articulated by writer, psychologist and mythologist Sharon Blackie.

What, if you were to be unflinchingly honest with yourself, do you already know needs to change?

If you were the director of the story of your life (*hint, you already are*) what directions would you give yourself so you can perform to the best of your abilities?

Tend to your soul by listening to and acting upon those longings that call to you and the images and themes that have fascinated you throughout your life.

Tend to these and they might just lead you to your calling – the unique gift you were born to share with the world in this life.

HER SOUL IS ABLAZE

Her soul is ablaze with anger.
Her soul is ablaze with holy rage.
Her soul is ablaze
And she is incandescent.
Burning in the refining fire
Turning all that is not just
To ashes.

Wait, and you will see her rise,
Phoenix-woman,
Smouldering with wisdom in her bones
Radiant with the power of her soul.

Her soul is ablaze
With fierce compassion and love.

Returning

RISING FROM THE ASHES

Phoenix is the mythical creature from ancient Greek folklore.

It is the long-lived bird who cyclically dies and regenerates.

In its mythology it is said that when its time has come, the Phoenix builds its own funeral pyre, and sets it and itself alight.

The old creature dies, and from its ashes a young, strong, regenerated Phoenix rises up, aflame with life and wisdom to begin a new, long life … and flies away to live it.

It is usually depicted in reds and oranges and golds; majestic and powerful.

It is a symbol of regeneration and of the sacred power of fire both to destroy and bring life.

Its spiritual teaching is that there is always a new beginning; we may be burned by our experiences, but we can always learn from them, then leave behind the past, and rise and grow into our true radiance and wisdom.

We all experience challenges and deaths: the ending of relationships; the dashing of hopes; the disappointment of failure, as well as the death of loved ones.

So, how would it be to invoke some Phoenix energy to access your power to rise and be reborn from the ashes?

May Phoenix inspire you with its healing powers of resurrection and renewal.

SOUL FIRE

I have a fire in my soul
That burns for truth.

I have a fire in my soul
That blazes with anger.

I have a fire in my soul
That is aflame for justice.

I have a fire in my soul
That could ignite a revolution.

I have a fire in my soul
That flashes and flickers,
Kindled by care for this hurting world.

I have a fire in my soul
Ignited by passion and pain
And it will never be extinguished,

For the fire in my soul
Is the sacred flame of love.

THE FIRE ELEMENT

Fire has a beauty which humanity has found hypnotic since we learned how to create and control it.

Whether it be in the hearth of a home or a candle flame or a bonfire, there is something transfixing about gazing into the dancing flames, isn't there? Something primal. Something which speaks to a visceral connection to our ancestors.

While it can be dangerous and destructive, the reality is, fire generates life.

Without the raging fires of the sun, there would be no life on Earth. Without the ability to make fire we cannot cook or provide warmth and shelter for ourselves.

Fire is dynamic. It is a catalyst for change, and it transforms all it touches.

And fire provides a potent metaphor for understanding our emotional, mental and spiritual lives.

It's the kindling of inspiration which sets a new idea alight.

It's the spark of insight that enables new ways of seeing a familiar topic.

It's the fire of courage giving you strength to act on your convictions and see things through.

It's the flame of authenticity which gives you the fuel to stand up for what you believe in.

It's the blaze of passion you may feel for a cause, a person, or a change you want to make in the world.

It's the hearthfire of love glowing within your heart with warmth and compassion for a partner, your family and friends, pets … and for all living things.

It's the alchemist's fire which, in changing base metal into gold, symbolically brings the unconscious to consciousness and transforms the individual's soul on its journey to wholeness.

It's the sacred fire burning in temples and places of devotion across the globe throughout time.

It's the spiritual fire that burns within that feeds your life force and guides you through life.

It's the soul fire that reveals your unique gifts and calling in this world.

And it is also the funeral pyre which burns the physical body, releasing the soul back to source.

Remember the element of fire when you feel dispirited, exhausted or indifferent.

Invoke the energies of fire by imagining you are stepping into a sacred healing fire that cleanses your aura of stagnant energies; an alchemical fire which reveals your gold.

Call on fire when you're feeling listless and lethargic and may it kindle the spark of life within you.

Let fire ignite your passion for life, for yourself, or for your lover.

Ignite the inner fire of courage when you need to face a fear.

Honour fire when you need some inspiration.

Returning

Whether it's with a creative project or whether you need a new way to approach an old problem, let fire ignite creativity within you.

Spend some time gazing into a candle flame and reflect on how you might honour the passions that burn brightly within your soul.

BRIGHT BEACON

Her anger
Burned bright –
Her trusted signal
That a boundary had been crossed,
A warning
To stand firm,
Her inner guide telling her
It's time
To say
NO.

She welcomed
Her anger
As a bright beacon
Shining in her life.

And she loved
How in honouring
This beacon-flame
She was helping
Inspire other women
To trust
Their own
Justified
Rage.

THE POWER OF ANGER

From a young age girls and women are conditioned to please others; to shrink to fit in; not to take up space.

This is why so many of us get stuck in the habit of people-pleasing and seeking external validation to prove that we're okay, that we're good enough, that we're worthy, even that we have a right to exist.

We're taught not to get angry.

And we're shamed if we do: labelled hysterical, a bitch, a witch.

We're afraid we'll get burned.

It's exhausting.

It is soul-destroying.

So, instead of being reduced to ashes by being ashamed of our anger, perhaps we might let our justified anger burn brightly.

What if we honoured our anger and listened to its messages?

What if we spoke our truth, and supported each other in doing so by listening, without judgment or offering advice (unless asked for)?

What if we learned how to channel and express our anger in ways that would bring about beneficial and much-needed change in our own lives and in our societies?

How wonderful that would be!

Can you welcome anger as the messenger – the bright beacon – it has the potential to be?

SOLAR POWERED

She's no longer
The little girl
Afraid
Of her own shadow.

She's now
The radiant woman
Blazing
With the power
Of the sun.

ADULT LIFE SKILLS

Sometimes no matter our biological age, we find ourselves acting like a child.

Having a tantrum when something won't go your way. Being snippy with someone who doesn't agree with you. Sulking. Name-calling. Telling lies. Bullying. Needing to be the centre of attention. Impatiently wanting your impulses gratified right NOW.

When we find ourselves regressing like this, it's a sign we're acting out needs from infancy or childhood which weren't met and we're viewing the world through a child's lens of 'it's not fair'.

Or, we might operate from a child-like sense of 'the world is unsafe' leading us to feel helpless, lonely, inadequate, ignored and left out.

Other times we're stuck in anticipatory dread of fearful experiences: of being rejected or laughed at; of saying the wrong thing or of being excluded; of losing a loved one or a beloved pet.

All of these are signs of the *inner child*: a living presence within your psyche. All that she experienced and felt is encoded in your nervous system. The fun and happiness, the confusion and fear, the joy and the sadness.

She needs to feel safe and loved so she can relax into the background and your adult self can run the show – which is how it should be.

So, if and when you find your inner child rising to the surface desperate or determined for her unmet needs to be fulfilled, it's beneficial to remind yourself that you're an adult now and you have more tools and greater emotional maturity and wisdom available to you than you did back then. You can cope differently.

As a child you were stuck when a bad experience occurred – you couldn't just up and leave. And children tend to feel things more intensely and don't have the language to describe it – it just feels horrible.

Children don't have a lot of coping mechanisms or inner resources to regulate how they're feeling – they rely on their parents and carers to help them regulate and feel safe. And if that support was unavailable or insufficient then dreaded experiences likely felt even more intense and perhaps even utterly overwhelming.

But as an adult, remember you have more control over your experiences and your environment than when you were a child – you likely won't feel as trapped.

You have the ability and wherewithal to remove yourself from situations that are not good for you; to argue your case; and to deal with challenging situations with more maturity.

Unlike in childhood, being rejected by someone else is not a life-or-death situation. Yes, it will be painful, but you're no longer a helpless infant utterly dependent on your carer. You can look after yourself.

Further, if something emotionally painful does occur, you won't feel it as keenly as when you were a child because you now have the ability to put it into perspective.

In addition, you have many more coping mechanisms at your disposal such as healthy distractions, friends or hobbies.

You can learn ways to help regulate your nervous system.

You can also bring the wisdom you've learned through your life experience to bear, and you can practise self-compassion.

While your inner child may sometimes feel scared and afraid of her own shadow – and she may rise to the surface more often than perhaps feels comfortable for you – remember that you are now an adult, with greater self-compassion, insight and resilience than you once had.

You are strong, capable and wise.

So can you close your eyes and feel her: this strong, radiant woman within you?

What does she look like?

What does she feel like?

How does she stand and move?

How does she speak?

How does she act?

How can you take a simple step to embody her today?

RESIST

Feel your anger, despair and grief
Because the toxic masculine that is patriarchy
Wants you numb.

Patriarchy wants you numb
Docile and unquestioning.
It wants you sad and frustrated
It wants you cynical and uncaring.

Patriarchy wants you numb
Because when you feel the intensity
Of your anger and rage
You will find at their core
A deep and fierce love
Of humanity and of justice.

When you let your anger burn
It will reveal
A power that gives you
The energy and strength
To say 'no, enough, not in my name'.

Patriarchy wants you numb.
So feel your feelings
As an act of resistance.

PATRIARCHY

Meaning 'rule of the father', patriarchy is the long-standing societal system of male supremacy.

Under this system, cisgender men (usually white and/or heterosexual, socio-economically privileged, able-bodied and religiously conservative) hold the positions of authority and power, are the arbiters of the rules of morality and the law, and hold social and economic privilege, including controlling land and property.

Its beginnings are complex and obscured in the mists of ancient history, though some say it began many thousands of years ago when the concept of 'fatherhood' took root i.e. when the male's role in females becoming pregnant was understood.

And thus began the control of female bodies and reproduction to ensure paternity of offspring was clearly established so that property, material goods and privileges passed down the patrilineal line, from father to son.

But however it began it has certainly been perpetuated through millennia of patriarchal religions with their 'God the Father' (and the exclusion of 'Goddess the Mother').

Its tentacles spread widely, and it seeks to shame, oppress and even destroy anything that does not look like it in order to keep its grip on power.

It oppresses men too in its narrow view of what it means to be 'masculine'.

It delineates and enforces narrow ideas of gender attributes and behaviour – false binaries that seek to keep us controlled and divided.

It has little space for nuance. It shuts down difficult questions. It shames difference. It belittles sensitivity and gentleness and kindness. It controls through shame.

It is profoundly misogynistic, racist, ableist, classist, homophobic and transphobic.

In many countries it is enforced through fundamentalist religious rhetoric and control.

It is certainly deeply embedded in capitalist economics where a few elite males hoard millions and billions off the backs of the work of the majority.

It is perpetuated by those who seek to control our culture. For example, look at the British tabloid press and the toxic misogynistic, racist, anti-immigration filth it publishes. And look at their owners who make billions off this poisonous trash and exert their malign influence over politicians who are scared to challenge them in case they become the next subject of their attacks.

I wonder how many of our unhealthy coping strategies are a way of trying to deal with the knowledge that the whole structure of society is not set up to support, value or reward people with our bodies (or skin colour, or sexuality, or identity etc.).

And ask yourself who does it suit for you to be self-critical and self-sabotaging, or to be numb and self-medicating through materialism and consumerism?

Who benefits from your turning inwards and embarking on an endless impossible-to-satiate journey of 'self-improvement'?

The agents of patriarchy, that's who.

Because if you think you're broken and need fixing you're less likely to look outwards and finally grasp how the whole damn system is set up to make you feel like a failure.

Yes, our emotional pain largely results from life experiences and in relationship with others. But patriarchy is the context in which all of this has arisen. It plays its part in your pain.

So I invite you to reflect on all of this.

And then do what you can to resist the life-denying soul-destroying hate-filled divisive conditioning of patriarchy.

And choose to feel.

Choose kindness.

Choose complexity.

Choose connection.

Choose life.

NICE GIRL NO MORE

No, I'm no longer the nice girl
Who bites her tongue to pieces
And smiles when she wants to scream
Who does her best not to rock the boat
In fear of capsizing and drowning in disapproval.

No, I'm no longer the nice girl
Because trying to be her was killing my soul
Strangling my voice
And leaving me gasping for air
Erasing my truth
And making me invisible, even to myself.

So no, I'm no longer the nice girl
Who craves approval and affirmation and love.

Now I am the blazing fire
The rooted presence
The truth speaker and seer.
I am the unapologetic woman
I was born to be.

ON NICENESS

It's still the case that girls and women are socialised to be nice and accommodating.

Don't rock the boat. Don't show off. Don't contradict.

Be kind to others and don't be selfish.

Put other people's feelings and needs first – there's a good girl.

I've lost track of how many women over the years have told me they feel guilty even thinking about putting their own needs first for once. Especially if they're mothers, who society expects to sacrifice their very soul for the privilege of doing all the labour of raising children and running the home and keeping the plates spinning for everyone else.

The definition of 'nice' is giving pleasure or satisfaction; being pleasant or attractive.

Notice that it's all about other people and *their* needs and perceptions.

There's nothing wrong with being respectful of others and accommodating when you need to be; there's nothing wrong with attending to your appearance if you want to; there's nothing inherently wrong with being attentive to other people's needs and feelings.

It is when you're constantly prioritising being 'nice' over being true to your own needs, desires, dreams and natural temperament that it becomes toxic.

Being overly nice can actually be a coping mechanism, developed in response to childhood experiences.

You'll likely have heard of the 'fight/flight/freeze' response to stress.

But there's also a fourth 'F' in these nervous system responses: the *fawn* response.

This is when, in response to threat or to avoid conflict, you immediately try to please the other person who is the source of potential stress.

This is often a response developed in childhood, where a parent or a significant authority figure is the perpetrator.

Children go into a fawn-like response to attempt to avoid the stress caused by emotional neglect, or to avoid abuse, by being a pleaser.

In other words, they pre-emptively attempt to appease their parent by agreeing with them, telling them what they know they want to hear, or by ignoring their own personal feelings and desires and doing anything and everything to prevent the ill treatment continuing[16].

This fawn response becomes a behavioural pattern that you will likely carry forward into adult relationships, including professional and personal interactions.

So, if you have an inner nice girl then please be kind to her because she's been trying to keep you safe by keeping you small.

But know that you can leave her behind in your past.

---

[16] Adapted from psychologytoday.com/gb/blog/addiction-and-recovery/202008/understanding-fight-flight-freeze-and-the-fawn-response

Returning

You don't need to be nice.

You are a grown woman now, with healthy needs and desires that you're entitled to get met.

You're a woman with informed opinions and valid feelings that you shall freely and unapologetically express.

You're a woman with goals and dreams that you will pursue without needing anyone else's permission.

Nice girl no more.

Woman. You are powerful.

And you are amazing.

ONE MORNING

*One morning
She woke up
And said
'Fuck it'.*

*And just like that
She stopped bowing
At the altar
Of what other people think
And she started living
Her life
As an act of daily devotion
To the truth and gifts
Of her soul.*

Returning

THE POWER OF SAYING 'FUCK IT'

What would you love to say 'fuck it' to in your life?

You don't have to say it out loud, unless you want to.

And I'm not suggesting you need to say it to someone else.

But saying it to yourself can feel immensely empowering.

It reminds you to be on your own side.

It acts as an affirmation that this is *your* life and, as you're never going to please everyone, you may as well please yourself.

It reminds you that you only live once so you may as well give something a go that scares you in case you regret it if you don't try.

It's irreverent and playful and helps you not to take life so seriously all the time.

I feel this 'fuck it' as an internal switch that I can flick.

It switches off fretting about what others might think and it switches on an inner source of rooted presence, self-compassion and grit.

How might your life change – both your inner world of emotions and thoughts *and* the external expression of yourself through your behaviour, words and energy – if you flicked this 'fuck it' switch?

How might you flick this switch today?

HAVE YOU HEARD HER?

Have you heard her yet?
The wild woman
The fearless feminine
The liberated lover of life.
Have you felt her yet?
The potent presence
The centred seer
The towering teller of truth.

If not, then fear not
For she IS within you
Ready to awaken
Ready to rise
Ready to rebirth you.
For she is the source
From which you came
And to which
You shall return.
She is life
Living itself
Through you.

She is your soul, woman.
Answer her call
When she begins to beckon
And step into
Your power and truth.

Returning

YOUR UNTAMED SOUL SELF

I believe we each have within us a part of ourselves that is untamed.

A part that is unbound by the 'shoulds' and 'should nots'.

A part of us who is wise and wild and free and who does not bow at the altar of what other people think.

Would you like to meet her? Your Untamed Soul Self?

Then follow the exercise below.

Take your time as you read through the words. Or you might like to record yourself reading them, with plenty of spaciousness between the instructions, and then listen back to be guided by your own voice.

*

First get settled and ground yourself. For example, have a stretch and shake out your shoulders. Take some deep breaths focusing on a longer exhale. Feel the seat beneath you … and the strong earth supporting you. Arrive here, in this moment.

And now, imagine you can see a full-length mirror ahead of you and you walk to stand in front of it…

You can see yourself in the mirror as you look today… Don't try to force or change anything… Look your reflection in the eyes… Look *deep* into your eyes…

And as you do so, you notice the mirror image changing… Slowly revealing your wisest, most confident and free self – your Untamed Soul Self…

She whose flames of truth and inspiration burn strongly and brightly... She who is undaunted... That part of you who calls you to speak your truth, to express yourself freely, to love and accept and value yourself... And to trust yourself... She IS there within you...

How does she look? What is she wearing? What's her stance? Her energy? Her facial expression? Take it all in... Whether it's details or impressions or feelings which come to you... You can't do this wrong.

Now, your Untamed Soul Self reaches out to you through the mirror, and you reach out to her and you hold hands... Feel her energy flowing into you... You are her. Strong and wise. Confident... Fully expressed... Free...

Feel her energy flowing into you... Coursing through your veins... Filling your heart... Touching your soul... Feel yourself as *one* with your Untamed Soul Self.

How would it be to know that you are her and that she is you and that you can call her to step forth whenever you need her...?

You smile at each in recognition...

Invite the felt sense of your Untamed Soul Self into your body and feel her untamed voice within you and ask ... what does she have to say today?

Breathe... And receive...

And what simple step can you take in the next 24 hours to anchor her presence or message into your life...?

...Now, slowly the mirror image of your Untamed Soul Self gradually fades...

Returning

And you see yourself reflected in the mirror once again as you are today…

But now you can see your Untamed Soul Self energy sparkling in your eyes and you can feel her energy in your body…

Welcome the presence of your Untamed Soul Self and her untamed voice in your body and soul…

And know that you can call on her to step forth whenever you need her energy and inspiration.

YOU WILL NOT SILENCE ME

You tell me I'm too much, too outspoken, too loud.
Get used to it. I'm not going away.
No. You will not silence me.

You tell me I'm aggressive, antagonistic and angry.
I have a lot to be angry about.
No. You will not silence me.

You tell me to calm down, to soften my voice, not to be so shrill.
My voice is a siren call for change.
No. You will not silence me.

You tell me to see the other side.
I've looked your way too long.
No. You will not silence me.

My ancestresses were silenced, raped and killed.
And yet I am still here.
No. You will not silence me.

Returning

REMEMBER YOUR ANCESTRESSES

Whenever you feel silenced – by your own fear or by the actions or words of someone else – remember.

Remember all those who came before you who could not speak; whose voice was silenced by the suffocating grip of patriarchal rules and crushing social norms.

Life for women throughout much of history has involved limited choices about where and how they lived, who they married, and how many children they bore.

They were voiceless. Gagged. Stifled. Suppressed. Their lived experience deemed unimportant. Their opinions disregarded. Their contributions overlooked. Their wisdom erased. Eliminated from *his*-tory.

Use this remembrance to motivate you if there's something you dearly wish to do in your life but feel scared to begin.

Remember their erasure when you find you're stopping yourself from speaking up. Recall their wasted potential when you're feeling fearful that you're not good enough.

Think of all the billions of women throughout patriarchal history whose dreams were extinguished or who never even dared to dream because it seemed so pointless to hope for a life outside the limited options available to their gender and social class.

And imagine your ancestresses cheering you on and applauding you, with pride-filled tears in their eyes, because you are fulfilling the dream that they dared not speak: the dream of freedom to live life on your own terms.

BIRDSONG

The next time you hear birdsong
Listen,
And take note.

The blackbird does not silence its truth
The crow does not worry that its voice is too loud
The robin fearlessly sings with full-throated glee
The chaffinch contributes its unique note with joy
And the sparrow chirrups with freedom.

You too have your own song to sing
Your unique voice to share.

So, the next time you hear birdsong
Let it be a reminder
To fly from the cage
And set yourself
Free.

AUTHENTIC EXPRESSION

The next time you have the opportunity, listen to birdsong (or find recordings online).

And listen with heartfelt attention.

Can you hear the pure freedom in the bird's song?

Can you feel its radiant glee?

Notice how the birds don't worry about being too loud or getting it wrong. They just sing. And each has its own unique song and pattern of expression.

Does it stir something within you? Arouse a yearning to express yourself freely?

How would it be to feel inspired by this freedom?

How would *you* express yourself?

It could be in your journal, or other written forms.

It could be through singing.

It might be voicing your true feelings to a loved one.

Or it might be through another form of creative expression.

What would you say?

What's been stopping you from expressing yourself fully and authentically until now?

What small, manageable steps can you begin to take from now on to express yourself more freely?

And what might change in your heart and in your life if you did?

MY SONG

If I were to sing
I'd sing of
Glittering wings
And things
Just felt and seen
At the edges
Of what I'm given
Permission to see.

If I were to sing
I'd sing of
Awkward truths
Bones in the shadows
And what hides
In the cave
Of what I thought
I shouldn't feel.

If I were to sing
I'd sing of
Veils lifting
And my rage
Shattering the cage
Burning the lies
Of what I've been
Led to believe.

If I were to sing
I'd sing of

The unseen threads
That hold me
In the web
Of the magic and mystery
And the truth
That life lives through me.

Yes.
I will sing
A song of
Vision and power
From the flower of my soul
To the bud in your heart
That we might
Recognise each other
And sing together.

YOUR UNTAMED VOICE

I believe that each of us is a divine, creative soul who has a distinctive voice and unique gifts to bring healing, inspiration and joy to this world – and that the purpose of our life is to uncover and express them.

And I know that when you unleash your untamed voice, you'll have a greater chance of finally living to your full potential.

But your authentic voice gets stifled by social conditioning that tells you to be a good girl and not to rock the boat and labels assertive women as aggressive and angry women as witches, as well as the layers of hurts and wounds experienced when younger.

And all of these serve to silence your true voice: the wise and wild voice of your soul.

My love you are perceptive, smart and creative.

It hurts when you know you've got something to share but you struggle to express yourself.

Perhaps you feel held back from expressing your true voice through procrastination, overwhelm and self-doubt (and maybe fear and anxiety too).

If you wish you could trust your vision and your voice and experience more ease, flow and magic in your life then you need to practise expressing your untamed voice.

And a simple and potent way to do this is through writing in a journal.

(Or you could create an audio journal by recording voice notes on your phone if that's more your thing.)

Take a moment to get in touch with your Untamed Soul Self (see p199), then write the prompt *'today my untamed soul self wants to say...'* and then let whatever comes up flow out of you and onto the page.

Don't edit; don't censor it.

This is for your eyes (and heart) only.

Other prompt ideas are:

Today my untamed soul self wants me to know...

Today my untamed soul self is longing for...

Today my untamed soul self wants me to...

Do this exercise regularly and discover the song your soul is longing to sing.

THE SOUL OF THE ROSE

The rose knows
Her place
In this world.
There is no doubt
In her budding
There is no fear
In her blooming
There is no worry
As she casts her petals to the wind
There is no questioning
In the sweet juice of her rose hips.

She is a rose.
And the rose knows
That she is here
To fully inhabit
Her rose-scented place
In this world.

This is her gift,
Her essence,
And her destiny.

What is yours?

PURPOSE AND CALLING

I believe that we are each of us born for a purpose and with a calling.

I believe that our purpose in life is universal: to grow and mature as a person and discover and embody our true nature, and in doing so serve the world and contribute to the sustenance of the web of life and the ongoing unfolding of the cosmos.

Our calling is the unique, individual soul expression and gift we were born to share.

In this sense, do you feel you are living your life on purpose? Are you aware of your calling? Now, I acknowledge it can feel intimidating to try to answer the question: 'what is my calling – what is my gift to the world?'. It's an enormous question! It may trigger feelings of inadequacy and unworthiness.

So how would it be to lean into the notion that each of us is here for a reason? That each of us has inherent value that does not need to be proved. That each of us is a unique combination of temperament, genetics, life experience, preferences and talents which means that we see things differently to others and express ourselves uniquely.

Can you see how this means that each of us has something of value to share with each other and with the wider world? That each of us is an individual and unique intersection in the web of life and that we are here because we're needed and that we matter?

And can you see that this means that *you* are needed and that *you* matter?

I believe that our soul is always speaking to us and has done so throughout our lives through patterns that recur again and again.

So, to attempt to discover your calling reflect on the images and themes and ideas that you're drawn to.

Consider what has always brought you joy and lifted your spirits.

Contemplate what comes so easily to you that you may overlook its significance because you forget that not everyone is as naturally skilled at this as you are.

Ponder the challenges that have arisen for you time and again.

Also reflect on what feels most painful in your heart – what might be called your 'core wound': a foundational mistaken belief which developed in childhood that you've carried with you ever since.

For example, that you're flawed and unlovable, that you're not good enough, that you're different from others and will never fit in or be understood, that you're ugly or stupid or dirty, that you're not wanted, that you must fix yourself in order to be acceptable, or that you don't have a right to exist.

This can lead you to your soul's calling.

Uncovering your deepest wound is soul work for, in the words of Sufi mystic Rumi:

> 'The wound is the place where the Light enters you'.

And, as painful as it may be, perhaps what you need to heal becomes the very thing you can help others with, in some way.

So I wonder whether when we're feeling anxious, low, or even depressed it is – at least in part – a sign from our soul that our life is out of kilter with its agenda. A sign we're off track. A warning signal asking us to stop and reorientate.

I've spent much time reflecting on this. I've considered what's challenged me throughout my life and the themes that have constantly recurred. I've also thought about what comes easily to me and my natural talents.

I am a highly sensitive soul who feels deeply but often finds it painful to do so. I've frequently felt desperately lonely and misunderstood throughout my life. I didn't receive the unconditional love, validation and affirmation I so desperately yearned for from my parents and it left a hole in my soul; a hole that I spent too long trying to fill from external sources. And because I'm naturally empathetic I know I'm not alone in feeling like this – I sense it in other people too.

I acknowledge that I have a natural gift with the written word and that what I share is heartfelt and inspiring and touches the souls of others. And I feel in flow when I'm writing, it brings me much satisfaction and joy.

And so, I believe that my soul's calling is to alchemise the emotional and spiritual pain I have experienced by sharing honest and tender words through my writing, in order to reach out and touch the hearts and souls of others who feel isolated and sorrowful, to help them know that they are not alone, and to help them heal.

This is my essence, my bloom, my destiny.

What is yours?

SOME GOOD FACTS

The sun is shining.
My cup of tea is warm and comforting.
This chair is strong and sturdy.
The scent of honeysuckle hangs sweet in the air.
And I am here, receiving it all.

These are just some of the good facts –
Simple blessings –
That today
I am choosing to take in, with gladness,
As a reminder
That here,
In this moment,
All is well.

TAKING IN THE GOOD

Our brains are hardwired to look for threats around us.

It's what's termed the *negativity bias* stemming from the millennia when early humans could easily have become lunch for predators. In other words, as we evolved over millions of years the brain became more sensitised to dodging sticks (threats) than chasing carrots (food or other satisfying things) because if you missed a 'carrot' you might lose out on lunch, but if you missed a 'stick', you might become lunch!

This negativity bias created an ever-present vigilance that kept us alive.

And our brain still operates in the same way now, even though, generally, the threats to our safety are not so life-and-death.

This bias is why, as modern humans, we remember the one criticism about a piece of work, for example, and forget the myriad of compliments.

As psychologist and author Dr Rick Hanson says[17], our brains are Velcro for the bad and Teflon for the good.

When we're feeling low or experiencing a dark night of the soul, this hypervigilance is heightened because we feel stressed by the intensity of the complex and challenging

---

[17] Visit rickhanson.net for a wealth of helpful articles, interviews, practices, courses and books all based around this principle and the principle that you can rewire your brain for greater emotional and mental wellbeing by taking in the good of everyday experiences and consciously growing the inner resources you need. This is known as 'positive neuroplasticity'.

emotions we're feeling, and don't know what to do with them.

Our inner world feels threatening.

The simple act of choosing to take in the good around you can help to level the playing field of the inherent negativity bias.

It's an invitation to notice simple good facts around you, that help your brain and nervous system to feel safe, contented and connected.

This isn't about walking around with rose-tinted spectacles nor is it an invitation to spiritually-bypass difficult feelings by sprinkling them with love and light.

No, instead it's about bringing balance.

For example, instead of being overwhelmed by grief, you can feel the grief *and* notice and receive with gladness the sweet scent of honeysuckle or your cup of tea or the safe sturdiness of the chair beneath you.

This is not to deny the grief (or the anger or the confusion, or whatever may be present for you), it's to broaden your awareness and open to the variety of experiences and feelings that are available to you each and every waking moment.

It can assist you in processing challenging feelings by helping you to feel a little less stuck.

Because when you sit with grief *and* gratitude, for example, rather than thinking it's a binary choice between feeling one or the other, the vice-like grip of the grief loosens.

And you realise that there is more in your inner world than grief.

You see how you can hold more than one feeling in your awareness.

When I realise this, I sense how I can hold my grief with a soft inner tenderness of self-compassion, and I relax a little.

I feel held.

I feel less alone.

This is a profound yet simple spiritual practice that brings great solace and yes, even joy.

Notice the everyday precious jewels of goodness surrounding you that help you to feel safe, contented and connected to the greater world of living beings.

Come home to peace, contentment and love.

DWELLING PLACE

This is my dwelling place.

My bones made of ancient stars
My body sustained by the sun
My heart enchanted by moonlight
My soul at one
With the ever-unfolding
Miracle
Of life.

DEFAULT MODE

It's easy to get stuck in 'default mode' – reverting to behaviour and attitudes that are familiar because they're your usual way of being.

The trouble is, sometimes your default mode is one that is not really in your best interests.

You may default to cynicism or bitterness. You might default to prioritising others' needs above your own – and to feeling resentful. You might default to feeling a victim or unworthy.

These kinds of default modes are likely a means of protecting your vulnerability, or guarding against anxiety or fears, arising from patterns created in childhood.

So it's worthwhile noticing what you tend to revert to. Because this is your dwelling place.

Now perhaps it is human to dwell on sources of unhappiness, anxiety, or dissatisfaction. It's the negativity bias kicking in that helps to keep us safe from threats.

But awareness of what we tend to dwell on, and our default mode, can help us to decide whether this is a place from where we truly wish to live.

If you were to ask me then I'd tell you that I tend to default to pessimism and dwelling in a shadowy place that is somewhat self-defeating. But if you were to ask where I'd *like* to dwell, well, the words in the previous poem express that! I'd choose to dwell in the numinous beauty of life.

So I ask you: where do you dwell? In the separation of sadness, fear and hurt? Or in embodied connection with the mysterious miracle of life?

THIS IS HOW I LIVE

I rest
In the lap
Of the Great Mother.

I walk
On the green mantle
Of Mother Earth.

I sleep
Amidst the soft starlight shimmer
Of the Milky Way.

I dream
Held by the deep peace
Of the Mystery of Life.

Returning

LIVING IN THE MYSTERY

Life and the cosmos are a great mystery. No human being has ever truly understood how it all came into being, why and for what purpose – if any…

The complexities of the human mind, heart and soul can seem impossible to understand. We can be a mystery even to ourselves.

Yet I find leaning into this mystery profoundly comforting. It reminds me that no matter what I think I know, I don't really know anything for sure!

And this prompts me to approach life with curiosity and an open heart. It puts my worries and woes into perspective. It reminds me to nurture the numinous and to look for the sacred in all.

It invites me to tend to the longings of my soul because that is the part of me which comes from this awe-inspiring mystery, and the part of me that will return to the mystery when this life ends.

And so I invite you to lean into the mystery…

Return to the web of life. Be held by the beauty below, above, around and within you. Be alive to the numinous presences that you can sense but can't see or name.

Be open to enchantment. Live in awe of life.

This is the joy that each moment can offer.

The heart-opening 'wow!' of realising you are a tiny yet unique and powerful part of this magical, miraculous cosmos. You exist. And you matter.

I Am With You

COME BACK TO YOUR HEART

Come back to your heart,
When your mind is racing
And you don't know which way to turn.

Come back to your heart,
When you're lost and lonely
And fear hope will never return.

Come back to your heart,
Even if it feels it's breaking
Through loss and grief and doubt.

Come back to your heart,
If anger blinds you
And you want to stamp and scream and shout.

For in your heart is strength and wisdom
To guide you along the way.

In your heart is love unwavering,
Bringing light to the darkest day.

In your heart is enough kindness and compassion
All fears and doubts to soothe.

In your heart is trust and connection
To help you see the truth.

Slow down, breathe and quietly listen

Returning

To the whispers of your soul.

Telling you that you are love and you are loved,
You are perfect, radiant and whole.

So, come back to your heart,
The centre of love within you,
Whenever you feel alone.

Come back to your heart,
The wellspring of healing within you,
And let it welcome you home.

HEART POWER

Understandably, much focus of health advice is placed on the physical heart organ, but never underestimate the role of the emotional and spiritual heart in contributing to your wellbeing.

The subtle heart is the source of our love and connection, but this source is also filled up by love and connection, creating a virtuous circle of healing.

The emotional bumps and bruises of everyday life that come with interacting with other humans can leave this heart power feeling somewhat depleted.

Periods of sorrow and grief, and heartache and loss, can leave your energetic heart feeling empty, numb or broken.

I've found that a practice of consistently connecting to my heart – especially in difficult times – is deeply comforting and reminds me that I am stronger, more compassionate and more connected than my fears and worries leave me feeling.

Here's a practice to connect with your subtle heart:

Place your hands over your heart. Soften your eyes. And breathe.

For a few breaths, imagine strength from the earth beneath you rising up through your body and filling your heart…

Now imagine light from the sun and moon and the sky above flowing down into your heart through the crown of your head…

Receive from source all the strength and love that you need.

How do you feel this?

Perhaps as a compassionate warmth spreading out from the centre of your chest; perhaps a sense of light and strength flowing up and down your spine…

Breathe and receive love, strength and compassion into your heart…

And let yourself sink into this feeling as it sinks into you… perhaps sensing it like sparkling motes of gold-dust, shimmering around you, flowing into the depths of your being and, in turn, flowing back out to share with the world…

*

Come back to your heart and live in connection with its loving strength.

Remember, you can call on it whenever you need to.

And know that your heart power is stronger than the fear that tries to protect you by keeping you alone and small.

HOME

And step
By step
Slowly
She walked herself
Home
To take
Her true place
In this world:
She walked herself
Home
To her soul.

COMING HOME

In dark times of inner turmoil and sadness, these words, from the Jungian psychoanalyst Marion Woodman, have brought me solace and inspiration.

I wonder if they will touch your soul too?

But if you travel far enough,

one day you will recognize yourself

coming down the road to meet you.

And you will say

YES.

May you walk yourself home to saying yes to yourself, and may you find the support you need to walk this road with presence and self-compassion.

Because all that you've been seeking was there all along, in the radiant, rich, multi-faceted depths of your soul…

WINGS

The chrysalis is opening now.
Can you feel your wings?
It is time to emerge,
To embrace your transformation.
Iridescent, unique, powerful.
Open to your full expanse.
And fly!

Returning

THE CHRYSALIS OPENS

Are you ready now to complete this journey of return?

You have descended and courageously spent time in the underworld, and perhaps for the first time you have seen there are gifts there and how to harvest them from this shadowy place.

But let's be honest, it's a challenging process, isn't it? It may have felt as if you didn't know who you were anymore or who you were becoming. It's a liminal state. It's messy. It's confusing. It's uncomfortable – painful even.

It hurts. But I think it hurts more to try and resist it.

It's like you've been in a chrysalis where the caterpillar of your old self broke down into mushy soup. But in this chrysalis, you've been reformed and now you will emerge, as the butterfly of your new self.

I wonder … have the words you've read in this book helped you to feel your newly forming wings?

This may not have been your first journey to the underworld, and it will probably not be your last – life inevitably comes with its share of challenges and sufferings.

But perhaps now you understand the process a little more. Perhaps now you can hold yourself with greater kindness.

Perhaps next time you will feel better resourced for the journey and know that in your heart you are courageous, you are compassionate, and you are ready … and you are never alone.

Fly, my beloved. Fly yourself home!

A BLESSING OF RENEWAL

May you find the courage to begin again.
May you open to see your path unfolding.
May you walk with hope and curiosity.
May you trust in your own potential.
And may you know
That you are worthy and that you are loved,
So you may rise, renewed.

CLOSING PRAYER

May I leave you with a prayer?

One that you might offer to Goddess, God, the Divine, a deity, the Great Mother, or the Universe, Source, the Cosmos, the Great Mystery…

Or maybe you might simply whisper it to your own heart and soul...

Please walk with me

Please give me strength and clarity

And eyes of truth

That I might see

My soul's path

Unfolding ahead of me.

May you walk through life feeling the presence of the many sources of support and love that are with you and within you, strengthened by the knowledge that you are not alone.

With much love and wishing you the blessings of tender and fierce self-compassion,
Stella x

WHAT NEXT

Thank you for reading. If you enjoyed this book then please consider leaving a positive review on Amazon, Goodreads or your favourite store.

*

Join me for *Simple Soulful Words*, my free weekly letter offering heartfelt and inspiring words that speak to your soul.

Simple Soulful Words is for people who value depth and sensitivity, reflection and seeking meaning, and sensing the sacred in everyday life.

Receive valuable perspectives, reflection prompts, practices and other helpful resources to gently guide you to greater self-understanding, inner peace and purpose.

Get inspiration to tend to your soul's whispers and longings.

Sign up or read/listen here:

stellatomlinson.substack.com

ACKNOWLEDGEMENTS

Thank you to all my teachers in the fields of yoga, meditation, mindfulness, energy healing, Goddess and nature spirituality, and neuroplasticity from whom I have learned over the years. Thank you also to the many writers whose books and wisdom I have steeped myself in on this journey, with a special thank you to those whose books I've read on understanding and healing the child within.

Thank you to Dr Rick Hanson for your books and courses – 'taking in the good' has changed my brain and my life!

Thank you to Dr Cheryl Cross who helped me to meet, listen to and love my inner child self who had felt abandoned, judged and lonely for so much of my life.

Thank you to 'Mr Schminkins' for visiting me nearly every day since summer 2022 and generously sharing your purrs, fluffy tummy and calming presence with me.

Thank you to both Judi and to Jyoti for your friendship, which I value so dearly.

And finally, and most deeply of all, thank you to my beloved husband Michael for your love, friendship, support and for always believing in me. I could not pursue this writer's life without you by my side, cheering me on. I love you beyond words.

ABOUT THE AUTHOR

Stella Tomlinson is an author, poet and Priestess writing about the emotional realities of life and finding spiritual support in nature.

She helps her readers awaken from the trance of unworthiness and tend to the longings of their soul so they can feel a greater sense of peace, purpose and fulfilment.

Her dearest wish is to help you feel less alone in this challenging yet enchanting journey that is a human life.

Stella's offerings draw on her own healing journey to self-worth and are based on almost 25 years' experience in personal and spiritual development through meditation, yoga, mindfulness, energy healing, menstrual cycle awareness, Goddess and nature spirituality, and positive neuroplasticity. She's been teaching and writing since 2011.

When she's not writing or reading, you'll find her walking in woodland, taking pictures, gazing at the moon, sipping gin, or hanging out in her tiny temple meditating, journaling or taking a yoga nidra nap.

She lives with her husband (and extensive book collection) in Hampshire, UK.

Connect with Stella via her website **stellatomlinson.com** and on Instagram, Facebook & TikTok
@stellatomlinson.author

Cycles of Belonging: Honouring ourselves through the sacred cycles of life

Cycles of Belonging is a guide to unlocking the powers of cyclic living to lead a more fulfilling, meaningful, and wholehearted life.

Discover ways to engage with the cycles of the breath, day, menstruation, the moon, the seasons and life for better emotional and mental wellbeing and to enhance your spiritual connection.

Cycles of Belonging guides you through six sacred temples:

- Presence - the breath cycle
- Daily Rhythms - the circadian cycle
- Sacred Blood - the menstrual cycle
- The Moon - the lunar cycle
- The Sun - the solar cycle, exploring the seasons and the wheel of the year
- The Life Cycle - exploring the female archetypes of Maiden, Lover, Mother, Queen and Crone

Let *Cycles of Belonging* take you on a journey home to wholeness, rooted deeply in the truth of who you are and the magical web of life that connects us all.

> *'A beautiful book on flowing in rhythm with the sacred cycles of life.'*

– Rebecca Campbell, bestselling author of *Rise Sister Rise*

Whispers From Mother Earth: Poems and prayers of healing, inspiration and transformation

Whispers from Mother Earth is a collection of poems and prayers that are a potent tool for healing and transformation.

In this book you will discover over 40 poems and prayers, reflecting different aspects of the Sacred Feminine:

- Goddess Whispers
- Blood & moon cycles
- Inner council of wise women
- Elements of earth, water, fire, air & spirit
- Soul

These compelling poems and prayers are suitable for reflective reading and to facilitate healing, inspiration and empowerment in women's circles, meditation groups and ceremonies.

'A precious gem. Ideal to remember your own connection with Mother Earth, your cyclical wisdom and the love of the Goddess.'

– Veronica Layunta-Maurel, The MindBody Reconnect

Peace Lies Within: 108 ways to tame your mind and connect to inner peace

In this book you will discover 108 practices, insights and inspirations to enable you to:

- Soothe your stress response using mindful body and breath techniques
- Feel balanced and calm by making friends with your emotions and mind
- Tune into the energy of your heart and soul to create meaningful connection

They are pathways to self-knowledge and self-acceptance, and greater compassion, inner peace and joy.

Bring these simple practices into your life and you will be amazed at your capacity to connect to the deep sense of serenity that lies within you.

If you often feel at the mercy of your mind and all those thoughts scrabbling for your attention, and yearn for inner peace, then this book is for you.

'To me this book is more than just a way to tame my mind, it offers a different perspective on living life with a greater sense of love, purpose and fulfilment.'

– Judi Craddock, author of
The Little Book of Body Confidence

USE OF THIS WORK

Stella loves seeing her work out in the world!

She is delighted for short quotes from this book – up to 200 words – to be shared as memes or in your own articles or books, provided they are clearly accompanied by her name as the author and the book's title.

She is also happy for the materials in this book to be shared in spoken or written form in places like yoga classes, meditation groups, women's circles and so on, or to be studied by book groups, discussed in classes, read from in ceremony, and quoted on social media as long as Stella is clearly referenced as the author and the title of the book is included.

If you share from this book on social media it would be great if you would tag Stella (@stellatomlinson.author) and use the hashtag #iamwithyou

If you require further clarification, please email stella@stellatomlinson.com

www.ingramcontent.com/pod-product-compliance
Lightning Source LLC
Chambersburg PA
CBHW071338080526
44587CB00017B/2885